James Murdoch

Ayame-San

A Japanese Romance of the 23rd Year of Meiji (1890)

James Murdoch

Ayame-San

A Japanese Romance of the 23rd Year of Meiji (1890)

ISBN/EAN: 9783744674096

Printed in Europe, USA, Canada, Australia, Japan

Cover: Foto ©Thomas Meinert / pixelio.de

More available books at **www.hansebooks.com**

AYAME-SAN,

A JAPANESE ROMANCE

OF

THE 23RD YEAR OF MEIJI (1890).

BY

JAMES MURDOCH, M.A.

ILLUSTRATED FROM PHOTOGRAPHS

BY

W. K. BURTON,

(PROFESSOR IN THE IMPERIAL UNIVERSITY OF JAPAN.)

REPRODUCED BY K. OGAWA'S

PHOTO-MECHANICAL PROCESS.

YOKOHAMA
SHANGHAI
HONGKONG
SINGAPORE

KELLY & WALSH, LIMITED.

1892.

PRINTED BY THE YOKOHAMA PRINTING AND PUBLISHING COMPANY, LIMITED.

I beg to acknowledge my indebtedness to Mr. K. Ogawa for some of the best illustrations in the volume; also to Professor C. D. West of the Imperial University and to Mr. G. Brinkworth for one photograph each.

So far as I am aware this is the first book that has been illustrated with true half-tone photo-mechanical reproductions printed with the letter-press.

W. K. B.

To G. B. Anderson, Esq.,

My dear Anderson,

In one of his bright and trenchant pieces of criticism Andrew Lang has vouchsafed the suggestion that 'some novelists of to-day would be much better, if they employed a friend to make objections.'

. I do not think it right to let this booklet go forth without putting on record my indebtedness to your objections—and still more to your sympathy—when I read the slips to amuse you during the eight weeks you lay spread-eagled on your back in a sick-bed in our Bohemian ranche at Omori.

J. M.

PART I.

I.

" Bonnie Charlie's noo awa
Safely ower the ragin' main
Mony a heart'll break in twa
Should he no come back again."

The two initial lines were given softly and with feeling, the third *crescendo* and the fourth which in the ordinary nature of things should have been the most tear-drawing of all, was all mixed and marred as to its pathos by a *fortissimo* that rolled rollicking up the trailer-clad cliffs, making them all re-echo the 'gain' in tones of sportive glee. This misguided and unsympathetic execution of the caudal appendage of the lament simply signified that the artist's soul approved of the cunning of his handiwork. He jumped his camp-stool back some half-dozen feet, and swaying over, paint-box in his right and brush in his left, he put his head on one side and looked critically at the piece of life his last few touches had summoned into being.

"Yes!" he muttered to himself. "I guess that will do. Let me see;—it's worth the best part of a matter of sixty dollars. Ten pounds for a morning's work is not so very bad considering the rest of the camp is still nothing but a chorus of snores. Oh! but it's a lazy country that Japan is, with a frightfully debeelitatin' effect upon men of even a verra strong moral fibre."

He put down his brush and paint-box and thoughtfully brought out a pipe from the breast-pocket of the pyjama-suit he was working in. As he cleared the stem and began to fill up he put his head on the other side and again set a-humming the lilt. He seemed to receive much joy from this second inspection, for the final line of the ditty rang out as if sounded forth from a war-trump.

Whizz! Crash! and a Japanese *geta* (wooden clog) flew past his ear and striking one of the stork-like legs of the easel in front of him dismembered the whole thing till it had the seeming of Poland after a partition treaty. He started up and turned round with something that sounded like a twin-brother to a curse.

"Confound you, you mad Irishman! An' dinna ye know that it's just a hundred dollars that this joke's going to cost ye,—twenty for the easel and eighty for the picture?" he blurted out, as with a rueful face not unruffled by anger he tenderly picked out the sketch from the litter on the moist sand. "Man, whatever possessed ye to wish a body good day in that fashion?"

"Day is it ye're talkin' about? Shure then, an' that's just pwhat is the mather! It's early cock-crow ye mane, an' here at all hours av the dead av noight, ye needs must go roarin' loike a dynamite blast in a tunnel an' gin'rally disturbin' the pase an' rist av an exhausted ship's company av wan wid that raucous raspin' yer misguided consate considers as so much heaven-born melojiousness!"

All this in a tumbling cascade of stutters and stammers, the words coming hustling and jostling against each other like a Japanese crowd at the railway turn-stiles. Also with the wickedest of humorous twinkles in a pair of eyes literally adance with mischief in spite of their owner's elaborately simulated sleepiness. He sat up rubbing them with his knuckles, and yawning like a landscape on which an adult earthquake is wreaking its will. Suddenly he dropped his hands and broke out into side-splitting mimicry of the artist's effort, trolling out

the Doric with a Hibernian brogue you could have
cut into slices with a jack-knife.

> "*Bonnie Charlie's noo awa*
> *Saaylin ower the ragin' maane.*
> *Mony a heart'ull break in twa*
> *Should he no come back again.*"

He rendered the ultimate notes with the roar of
an infuriated bull charging a red rag. Then he lay
back in screams of mocking laughter, the long
pendant tassels of the buccaneer-like night-cap
wherewith he was adorned as to his head, vibrating
and quivering as they accentuated and punctuated
the peals. At last he threw the *futon* (quilt) aside,
and jumping up off the mats, came out on the sand,
where the painter had already addressed himself
to fishing up the wreckage of his friend's handiwork.

His advent contributed a picturesque addition to
a picturesque landscape. His nightcap as already
insinuated was in itself a work of art. But it was
dwarfed into insignificance by the gorgeous *yukata*
in which he was swathed from the shoulders downwards. It was all over snakes and centipedes and
dragons and devils; it only lacked a bottom fringe
of leaping flames to complete all the reminiscences
of a fine old Spanish auto da fé. As it stood, it was
eloquent of delirium tremens. It was kept toge-

ther at the waist by a huge black leathern belt such as you see in illustrated story-books about pirates.

"'Mony a heart'ull break in twa!'" he went on scathingly as he came forward into the sunlight. "An' it's just loike yer North British consate to think that all the petticoats an' purty gurls in Japan 'ull black their teeth and go into mournin' when your moightiness is plazed to widdraw the loight av yer ugly count'nance from shinin' upon thim. Don't yez know the sole an only regret they'll have in conniction wid your unholy mim'ry 'ull be on account av the baad money ye've doubtless thraded off upon thim?"

The painter made no immediate reply. He was anxiously scanning his overturned water-colour. At last he put it carefully aside with a sigh of relief and then he turned him to uprear his fallen and dismantled easel.

"Well," he remarked at last, looking up from tightening a screw after a minute's pause, "I'm thinking my models *quâ* models will be a bit sorry maybe. Speaking from a strictly business point of view———"

"Models *quâ* models and a strictly business pint av view!" mimicked the other. "As if an artist's immortal sowl lived on models *quâ* models and a strictly business pint av view alone! Why, you ould dhrumskin av money an' maxims, you've no more sintimint than a Japanese woman. An' I can't say worse than that."

"Well, you're maybe no verra far wrong there, —in the latter part of your discourse," replied the Scot cautiously. "The first being a wee bit personal, we'll not discuss it. But the female portion of the Mikado's subjects remind me not remotely of how my great-grandfather found the Duke of Buccleugh's port wine. 'It's a fine drink, an' a braw drink, yer Grace,' said he, 'but a body never seems to get ony forrarder on't.' In the satisfaction of a man's soul those Japanese women leave much to be desired."

He relapsed into silence as with brows wrinkled into furrows he again bent him to splicing a broken leg of his easel. His companion retreated to the verandah, and sitting down on it, leant back and stretched into the room for a pipe browned and seasoned to the sheeny blackness of soot. He took out his tobacco pouch and began to fill up with all the care of a devotee handling a real genuine chip of the True Cross. At last he put it between his lips, struck a match and lit up. Then he lay back with his head on his clasped hands, smoking like Oshima in the offing and uttering never a word. The painter was equally eloquent as he went on tugging and knotting and splicing.

It was at Misaki in the summer of 1890. Right in front of the mill-pond they mis-name the harbour is a huge misshapen lump of an island, giving one as O'Rafferty alleged, the idea of an abortion that has got over the diseases of infancy and reached the stage of hobbledehoydom. It is hard to say what purpose Providence had at the root of its wisdom teeth when it dumped it there. O'Rafferty says it was clearly meant for a short-distance sailing course, but then on a matter of this sort his opinion is really not worth half the price of a second-hand pair of braces. Among his numerous weaknesses of the flesh is an undue fondness for salt-breezes; boats in his category of the needs of the soul being placed far above whiskey and immediately after tobacco. He tells with a gleam in his eye and a twinkle in the back of the head— there usually is a twinkle somewhere in that neighbourhood when O'Rafferty assumes an extra thick brogue for purposes of confounding common-sense —he tells how 'a dipytashun av two faymale missionary wimmen' once waited on him "tu rimonstrate wid him on the reckless way he was jeopardising the immortal part av him.' Their text seems to have been systematic Sabbath-breaking on the High Seas, and a declaration from O'Rafferty that if he 'wint up aloft and found the saints had no interprise in the way av periodic sailin' races, he

would petition the Authorities for a special passport
to let him navigate an asbestos 27 rater on the
Lake av Brimstone below.' So on a matter of this
nature his opinion doesn't count.

The seaward slope of the lump is overgrown
with bamboo grass and dwarfish shrubs, all apparently the victims of a fixed idea to escape from
the raking winds that come blustering up from the
Bonin Islands, for they've all got their backs to the
sea, and bent double like so many sprint runners
toeing the mark on the strain to catch the pistol-
crack of the starter. Its easternmost scaur is topped
by a light-house that keeps up a persistent and in-
discriminate flirtation with all the ocean-craft

that get inside of Ōshima. After dark it brazen-facedly ogles them with all the power of its discs, varying the performance with soul-perturbing utterances from its vocal organs when the fogs and the night-rack come swirling upwards in smoky drift from the surface of the deep, and writhe about its reflectors like a school of disembodied spirits suffering, as O'Rafferty puts it, ' from uneasy consciences and a powerful indigistion.' Right under the light-house on the landward side was a little Japanese summer-house. It overlooked the long slit that formed the harbour, with its fleet of fishing craft and fringe of houses straggling along the bottoms and backwards up the slopes of the trailer-clad bluff vis-à-vis. It was in this shanty that they had their head-quarters.

They were two in number, for the *sendos* and *boy-sans* they had with them form no integral part of the story.

In the first place there was O'Rafferty. Till the moment he was named by his name, and spoke for himself, he might have been writ down as anything, always saving and excepting a Sassenach. He was passing dark and swarthy, with the olive tint you find in Mediterranean lands. His nose might have been come by feloniously,—purloined from the illustrated playbill of some Japanese theatre addicted to the representation of old-time

Daimyo life. It was flanked by a pair of eyes almond-shaped enough to pass for Mongolian, and sufficiently agleam with fun to be reckoned among the belongings of a Milesian. But as soon as Mr. O'Rafferty was introduced by name, and uttered himself in what *he* mistook for English, there was no mistaking *him*. His father was a lineal descendant of an ancient Irish King, and from the age of ten down to the day Phelan had sailed in the troop-ship for Bombay, brogue and brogue only had sat upon his lips. As he put it himself, it was " wan av the Japanese county families that was risponsible fur the faymale part av his ancistry." His father had married her when in garrison at Yokohama, and

hence it was that O'Rafferty was so wonderfully
Japanese-looking when he donned the costume of
the country, and so peculiarly proficient in the
vernacular of the land wherein he was now a
sojourner. For although he had left off ordering
servants about in Nihongo when he lost his mother
and went home to live with an uncle of his, a
retired naval officer at Waterford, he found the
re-conquest of his mother's tongue no very difficult
task when he returned to Japan two years before,
—in '88. He had lived with this uncle till eighteen,
and it was this old salt that was chiefly accountable
for O'Rafferty's moral twist in the matter of
yachting. Then he went to T.C.D. and was
just on the point of going out B.A. when he set
sheep's eyes on a commodore's widow old enough
to be a junior aunt to him. For a long time she
gave him encouragement but finally she threw him
over for a Dean in gaiters. Hereupon O'Rafferty
promptly and diligently sought out the "dirthiest
rigimint av bla'gards tu be found in the service an'
jined them." He meant this as a "double-barreled
blast av contimpt," partly at the expense of the
former naval connections of the widow, and partly
at religion and respectability as sheltered under a
shovel-hat. Anyhow that was O'Rafferty's explanation of the incident and he sometimes does
speak the truth. He was shipped off to Afghan-

istan and thence to Egypt and the Soudan.
O'Rafferty developed into a great shot and a mighty
warrior and as a slayer of men soon took rank
immediately "afther the rigimintal saw-bones." As
a reward he rose to sergeant, but he was reduced
"for allowin' his better feelings to run away wid him
an' takin' pity on a pore Egyptian Pasha whose
health was sufferin' all along av totin' an excissive
load av useless goold rings and jewelry around on
his dilicate person." And then when he got as far as
lance-corporal again he was once more "rejuiced
fur accidentally upsettin' an orf'cer wid wan leg."
By this time his six years were almost up and then
what happened must be told in O'Rafferty's *ipsis-
sima verba*, as he told it to his friend Gifford.

"Ye see, I'd come down from the front to Suakim
where there was a lot av monimintal corn-shtalks
from Australia. Although they didn't do any
foightin' tu spake av, they were men av no mane
courage, otherwise they'd never have vintured their
bodies on such outrajisly tinder shupports as their
legs was. They killed wan donkey they mistuk fur a
shpy, an' that was all the damage they did tu the
inimy an' the inimy didn't do even as much tu thim,
no doubt being moighty afraid av tacklin' the ragin'
typhoon av profanity their kyamp allus was. But
they had their parson all the same, an' he prached
av' a Sunday. So whin I came down from convertin'

the haythen wid ball cartridge an' the butt av a rifle I wint tu hear him, bein' moindfull av a little harmless divarsion. His tixt was 'Blessed are the pase-makers fur they shall be called the childer av God',—which shtruck me as moighty queer doctrine fur sodgers. He prached wid an accent that was first cousin tu a Cockney coster-monger a-callin' ''Ot pies! Pies all 'ot!' an' some av the Surrey Rigimint that had dhropped in tu pass the toime av day wipt tears av home-sick affection. Well, he pershuaded me, and whin I wint out I saw two New South Welshmen in the midst av an argument wid fistes. I thried to stop ut, an' wan av thim thanked me fur me throuble not by callin' me a choild av God but by a relliction on the morals an' the natural history av me muther. Her son, spite av all the prachers in the wurruld, couldn't stomach *that*, so I just named him by the name av a bla'gard an' tould him to do his wurrust. Afther the siventeenth round there was'nt a gasp av wind left in the wan to compli- mint the other on his performance. So we shuk hands an' adjourned tu the cantheen, an' since that day to this we've been as thick as a pair av twins born out av wedlock. When I got me discharge he tuk me wid him tu Australia an' put me in the Broken Hill Silver Mines. Wan Monday we bought the scrip at sixpence an' the followin' Sun- day it was at £2, an' we were wurruth a mather av

£20,000 a piece. Then not bein' good enough fur a
Praste nor bad enough fur the New South Wales
Parlimint, I came up to Japan tu build a yacht an'
tu be somewhere where I could keep cool. For
ever since the Commodore's widdey bruk me heart
I've been doin' nought but sizzlin' an frizzlin' in hay-
then cloimes loike a plucked turkey rehearsin' fur
Christmas."

Then there was Gifford. He was a Scotchman by
birth, an American citizen by adoption, and an artist by profession. He was retained by a New
York magazine that had sent him forth to illustrate
the world for it on a salary considerable enough to

make an am-
bassador
from a smal-
ler court
wickedly
and unchari-
tably en-
vious. Since
the day he
had signed
an engage-
ment with
its proprie-
tary he had
been mostly
everywhere.
His sketch-
es covered
nooks of the
Old World from Tangiers even unto Vladivo-
stock and from the Cape up to St. Petersburg. He had just come off an overland trip
through Siberia and was now putting in the
ultimate week of a three months sojourn in
Japan. This stay was wantonly and flagrantly in
defiance of instructions from head-quarters; some
of the happy family on the continent of Europe had
just then been snarling at each other in a way that

looked rather more like business than usual and
Gifford had just got his second telegram imperatively
ordering him off to the probable place of argument.
But he wanted to enjoy the luxury of Japanese
cleanliness for a season after his nine months over-
landing through Russian and Mongolian dirt, at the
same time being wishful for the advantage of another allowance of entertaining and profitable com-
munion with his old friend O'Rafferty.

They were friends of five years standing and
their first happening on each had been in Ethiopia.
It was at a spot where the great pea soup like Nile
flood breaks into a series of foam-tipped lashers.
Their sullen roar was the only sound that broke
the parched aridity that vanished into space on
both sides of the watery furrow that intersects it,
and the stink of the Nile mud the only aroma that
flavoured it.   In the middle of the stream was a
dhow that had been fool-hardy enough to try con-
clusions with a sunken ledge of basalt. The rock
had torn open her bottom even as a rhinoceros
horn rips up the belly of a horse and she was
sick unto sinking.   O'Rafferty was just in time to
see her disappear in the welter of waters, and to
lend a hand in fishing out the sole white man she
carried from the bed of Nile mud to which he had
swum for refuge.   O'Rafferty had his reward; he
never before heard such swearing as that man then

indulged in. It turned out that the Irishman had just assisted at the untimeous obsequies of six months work, obtained at the price of hunger and thirst, untold bodily discomfort and manifold risk of sudden death. It was a case that admitted of sympathy, and O'Rafferty was sympathetic by nature. The artist groaned inwardly as he mourned the best subjects he could ever find in life. O'Rafferty told him to pull a stiff upper lip and to come with him and see sights. He accepted the invitation and went. They had been in several squares together with a few odd thousand dervishes yelling murder all round them, and thoroughly meaning it. Each had got the other out of more than one tight fix and as a consequence their friendship waxed thick. So when one March morning O'Rafferty spotted the other on the Yokohama Hatoba "disguised in a clean shirt loike a gintleman an' a dacent mimber av society," there were great doings that same evening in the Treaty-Port. Once more O'Rafferty told him, 'to come and see soights' and again Gifford gave heed unto him. But the sights he now saw were not as the throbbing panorama of the hurly-burly life of the desert and Gifford's soul was beginning to be sick of their tameness.

In company they had hied them forth to spy out the nakedness of the land and to limn its life in all the nooks where globe-trotters most do congre-

gate.   And now here they were, enjoying a peace-
ful rest at Misaki, waiting for the sailing of the
American mail-boat three days later on.

II.

For some minutes the deep calm of the morning remained unbroken by anything save the slow and luxurious "puff! puff!" of O'Rafferty's meerschaum, and the shuffling of the artist's feet as he proceeded laboriously with his repairs. At last the Irishman removed his pipe from his lips and took up his parable :—

"It's moighty aisy tu see that the American hasn't kilt the Scotchman in ye, at all, at all! Think av any sinsible man fiddlin' wid that thing fur tin blissed minutes as you've done. It's a waste av toime, tu say nothing av the discouragemint it is tu the industhry av easel-making!"

"Man!" replied Gifford through his clenched teeth—he was using them as a third hand to hold a piece of string.—"Man, ye know nothing of the virtue of thrift."

"Well now, that's just pwhat tickles me! Tu

hear ye spake, wan would think your parents had mint yez fur the superlative av maneness. But ye aren't a mane maan, as I know. When it comes to the sittlemint av a reckonin' ye do your share av the wurruk. But at the same toime ye always begin an interprise wid an estimate that descends tu the most inconsid'rable trifles. Ye seem tu do it as a moral duty. No doubt it's the outcome av yer misguided choildhood, being as a Scotchman and a Presbyterian dhragged up on the Multiplication table and the Shorter Catechism. Fur instance, your conduct wid yer models is atrocious!"

"I guess I always pay them squarely, anyhow," replied Gifford drily with a vicious tug with his teeth at a knot obdurate to the undoing of his fingers.

"Thim's my very wurruds! But ye begin by screwin' thim down till their nakedness costs ye less than nothing a yard per hour, and then when ye pay thim ye disgorge loike a dyin' thafe makin' his pase wid the Church. An' they aren't wurruth it, and ye only raise the tariff and shpoil the thrade fur better men that come afther yez."

"There!" said Gifford at last setting up his reconstructed easel with a sigh of relief. "Man!" he went on, "what you say about thae models is nearer to the truth than you maybe usually get. They are'na worth it,—they're *most* unsatisfactory."

"Shure an' pwhat's the matter wid thim?"

queried O'Rafferty, knocking the ashes out of his meerschaum, and with an extra twinkle in his eye.

"Matter! Everything! They're just like Japanese fruit, fair enough to look at externally, with all their paint and powder and hair-pins and sashes on, but nothing at all when you peel off the covering and come to the kernel. They are just like the earth in the beginning,—without form and void. It looks as if the Lord got tired of his job soon after taking them in hand and—

"Shtruck for a rise av wages," put in O'Rafferty with the bowl of his pipe in the tobacco-pouch again upon his knees.

"— left them with an arrested development," went on the artist paying no heed to the profane interruption. "I haven't seen a female in Japan with any approach to lines, or proportion, or bodily grace, or symmetry at all!"

"Well, then I don't think much av yer eye-sight, if thim's your sintimints. Now if ye'd just luk at my gurl!"

"Your girl!" interrupted Gifford with astonishment.

"That's pwhat I said! Don't yez understand the Widdey's English? If ye'd luk at my gurl—and she's Japanese entoirely—you'd see grounds tu amind yer opinion. Loines, an' grace an' symmetry an' all that, is it? Well then, if ye'd just luk at her

head and her waist, it's just loines you'll be seein,'
me son! Then when she's in stays—

"In stays! Oh Lord! A Japanese girl in stays!
Laced in front most likely and the top where the
bottom should be, and the whole thing over
her bodice!"

"— she's grace itself. An' then when she runs—

"Waddles, you mean!" corrected the unsympathetic Gifford.

"—it's just the poethry av motion she is. An'
if ye examine the curves av her stern—"

Gifford almost dropped his bush in open-mouthed
astonishment. All his facial muscles were con-
centrated into one great stare of horrified wonderment.

"Come now, O'Rafferty san! Don't you think
what you suggest is a trifle indelicate, not to say
positively indecent."

"Indacent yersilf! It's grace and proportion
an' symmetry an' the loines av a Venus da Milo
she has, and more besides. There's not the loike
av her widin the four seas av Britain, nor even on
the wathers av Ameriky!"

"Why to believe you, you have struck a regular
Komachi!

"And *Komachi* it is, me son! An' shure she's
wife and sister an' choild, an' all tu me and I luve
her wid a luve passing that av woman. And there

she lies bobbin' in the shtream and wid the glorious
sunlight makin' a picture av her that's mate fur a
man's soul tu luk upon!"

"Why, O'Rafferty man, you're a poet!" said
Gifford when the other came to a pause in his
impassioned flow.

"An' is it only now that the immortal fact
begins tu dawn upon yer benoighted ignorance?"
replied the Irishman with contempt.   "Who was it,
I'd loike tu know, that made all the pomes for the
barrack-room av the rig'mint if 'twasn't Phelan
O'Rafferty? An' many's the dhrink av good liquor
thim pomes have brought me!"

"Well I hope it was something with human
interest about it that inspired them. For me, I
don't see what there is to go wild about in a wheen
of soulless, inanimate boats. They're only one

degree less interesting than a Japanese woman. If it were art now,—landscapes, or figures, or fighting, or love-making or drinking I could understand it. And of all these five it's only the first and the last that count for anything in Japan; for the scenery is fine and the whiskey is only fourteen pence, there being merely a five per cent *ad valorem* duty on the liquor."

O'Rafferty did not deem these remarks worthy of any reply. He again threw himself back on the verandah while Gifford sat down beside him, evidently in a reflective mood.

"If it hadn't been for you, O'Rafferty, ma friend, he said at last, 'I'd have been bored to death in this most over-rated of belauded countries. The first week you think you're in Paradise, and if you quit then, the chances are you will weep with regret. But three months of it! I begin to repent of my insubordination to the authorities. But the *China* sails on Saturday and in Japan, Phelan O'Rafferty is the only thing I haven't seen enough of."

"Shure an' it's yoursilf that has kissed the blarney-stone!" said O'Rafferty without any movement further than a confidential wink at the ceiling.

Gifford removed to his camp-stool and for some minutes sat with his chin in his hand and his elbow on his knee, looking out over the stretch of water below them, just beginning to stir with all the life of an awakening fishing-village.

" Je-ru-sa-lem ! " he suddenly burst out darting up as if some one had shot a dozen volts of electricity into his spinal column.

" Mother av Moses !" remarked O'Rafferty, as he picked up the seat the artist had overturned, " An' its no cowld-blooded maan yer own mother's son is. You're impulsive to a degree upsettin' to a kyampstule, and outrajisly discomposin' to a frind's moral feelins. As for them fleas now——"

" Fleas, be——" returned Gifford with an impatient wave of his left hand behind him. " I wish you'd ease off your jawing-tackle for the tenth part of a jiffey. It's Komachi herself in the very flesh that's over there, or at all events a younger sister of hers, and at the same time one that could give her points ? "

It was plain that Gifford was unduly excited ; he forgot to be nasal, as he usually became when he waxed oracular.

O'Rafferty also jumped up. He followed Gifford's eyes across the stretch of blue beneath them to the cliffs on the other side of the harbour entrance. It was on a *furoba*, or detached bath-house in the compound of one of the villas on the ridge that they rested.

" Peepin' Tom av Coventhry !" ejaculated O'Rafferty with well-simulated scorn and contempt when he perceived the object of his friend's rapt and

hungry gaze. But notwithstanding he looked as
eagerly and intently as the artist himself.

"Shure, an' its mesilf that am ashamed av'
yez! Don't yez know the pore gurl 'ud be
blushing a red rosy pink in every inch of her purty
anatomy if she thought the sacrilegious oiyes of
irriv'rint foreigners were strayin' all over her unadorned person widout a passport from the lawful
authorities?"

Gifford's only reply was to take up his binocular
and bring it to bear on the spot. He looked for a
full three minutes and then he put it down with something that sounded like a gasp.

"If that's a Japanese woman I take back every
one of the ungracious remarks I made in my folly
a quarter of an hour ago!"

"And it's a moighty foine ornament fur the stule av repintance ye'd make! A Japanese woman! Av course it's a Japanese woman. In your innocence, ye thought it was a Japanese maan didn't yez?"

"What a bust!" broke out Gifford heedless of O'Rafferty's sarcastic prods. "What lines, and what a poise! I've often dreamt of such a woman, but this is the first time I've seen her in the very flesh."

"Wid no clothes on tu speak av at all, barrin' nature's own iligant and excillint raimint," went on O'Rafferty scathingly. "It's a modest young man that yer own father is risponsible fur!"

"It's a hundred dollars a month I'd give her to pose for me! Only my beastly luck as usual! Only three more days here, and what could a fellow do in three days with *her*?" went on the artist in a tone of petulant despair.

"Do wid her? Nothing, me son, and that's short an' sharp an' compenjous! An' three months, or even three years a-top av yer three days wouldn't change the score. Don't yez know there are Japanese women *an'* Japanese women, just as there are artists *an'* artists. An' do you think in yer stupenjus vanity that she'd feel flattered at yer offer? Go an' make it, an' I don't say they'll kick yez out at the door, because in the first place ye'll niver get in, an' in the next they're polite, an' in the third their toes are tinder, but ye'll have yer nose put so much awry that wid that as a further set-off to your own natural inherent ugliness ye darsn't show yer face in society for a week av Sundays. Don't yez know that thim ould-toime Japanese are as proud as the Divil afther his fall, and that that ould painter gintleman, her uncle, wid just up and quarter yez into three halves wid as little compunction as he'd dismimber an onion?"

"Painter is he?" asked Gifford with great interest.

"Thim's my wurruds! Do ye think there was no artist in Japaan till yer mightiness came along? Or maybe ye think the breed is extinct loike the sword-smiths, or the Phoenix? 'Twould just be in keepin' wid your misguided uneducated foreign notions av the counthry. Yes, me son, 'twas a painter I said, and besides he's a swordsman, an' ye'd better think twice before you go philanderin' over wid yer indacent proposals fur models an' dirthy money in that quarter!"

Gifford put an elastic band in his mouth and began to chew it reflectively.

"And as for foreign gintlemen gettin' a wurrud wid the gurl it's simply out av all question. Even wid *thim* it's impossible, and as fur itinerant vagabonds loike us, it can't be done at all, at all. There's Frobisher av the Legation, an' Wilson av the Department av

Justice and Somerville the big Yokohama merchant,—they've all thried till their backs bruk to
get on spakin' terms wid the gurl, but never a
wan av thim cud get widin hail av her stern-sheets.
It's just the same as wooin' the side av' a mountain.
You see she knows a thrifle av English besides
bein' a clipper tu start wid."

"Knows English! How is that?"

"A faymale missionary woman tached her. Her
father was killed in the Satsuma war, and so was
her cousin, that old gintleman's son. An' he just
tuk charge av her and her mother, an' also av the
youngster that came along posthumously afther his
son's desase. He's spint all his earnings on thim ;—
at least that's pwhat that ould screw av a Chinese
quack doctor down there sez, an' he should know,
fur he knews everything most, barrin' his own profession. And he had in a faymale missionary tu
tache thim a sinsible and Christian language, fur
the Japanese tongue is like most av the other institutions av the counthry, all up-side down, wid
the head av a sintence where the tail should be, an'
the beginnin' av a buk at the end, an' the whole
thing a colliction av Hieroglyphics an' Haythenish-
ness. An' the bhoy is Santaro, the little chap that
draws himsilf up as shtiff as a post salutin' on
parade and then wid a tin-acre smoile on his expanse av chubbiness lisps out 'Good-day! Where

are you going.' He's a foine little *botchan*, (little boy)
and the chances are he'll grow up tu be a maan,
bein', as he is, moighty fond av boats, an' ships an'
the things av salt-water gin'rally. An' by the token,
it's him that's gettin' into *Komachi's* dingy just at
this very moment! An' off he is, the little divil,
scullin' like a Thames waterman! An'—Halloo, yez
ould bundle av fat an' politeness wid a yawnin'
abyss av darkness fur a mouth, an' pwhat is it me
insignificance can do fur yer honourable silf? An'
honorably early, honorably it is!"

The last section of O'Rafferty's remarks was addressed to an old lady of any age between forty and
fifty who then came up with her face wreathed into
the set smile of a Japanese either about to ask for
something or to say something particularly nasty
and disagreeable. She kept on bowing and bob-
bing and smiling, and at last began a long rambling
recital punctuated by explosions of uneasy cackling
laughter. Gifford merely caught something that
sounded like *Osore-irimashta* (overcome with awe),
and that was because it always came round like a
circulating decimal in a sum.

O'Rafferty listened and nodded and said "*Hei !*"
and "*Ha!*" and "*So desu ka?*" in the most approved conventional style till the story ran itself
out, and then he turned to the artist.

"An' it's mesilf that am ashamed av yez! An'

afther all your foine diclamation about squareness tu
your models! Do yez know that it's orphans an'
widdeys ye've been exploitin' all the toime worse
than a millionaire cotton-lord?"

"What's the meaning of the rigmarole?" asked
Gifford a little impatiently.

"Just that ye've been robbin' the widdey an'
the fatherless! Didn't yez have three av the off-spring
av this pore ould lady tu pose fur yez, and didn't
yez pay fur two only? Possibly ye wanted thim
at a riduction for quantity, but that don't go in
Japan,—not even if yez were tu hire a theayter-full
av thim."

"When was that?"

"Whin? The ould lady sez yesterday, whin ye
got all the gossoons av the village tu dishport them-
silves wid nothin' but their summer clothes on in the
wather. Yez owed the ould lady three cents and ye
docked her wan fur reasons av economy no doubt!
Now I think ye'd better shell out, or shall I do it fur
yez? Ye see, I'm risponsible fur the ripytashun an'
unpaid debts av me friends in this counthry as I
tould yez when I put yez up at the Club."

Gifford's ears were open to the remonstrance
and he paid the deficiency. The old lady bowed
herself out with a flood of *arigato gozaimasu*'s
(Honourably thank you's) streaming from behind
the barrier of her blackened teeth.

" Now then, me son, you can rist wid a clean
conscience till nixt toime. Ye've paid your debts
and contributed wan more cent to the hoard av
that ould miser av a Chinese quack-doctor av a
usurer ! "

"Explain !" said Gifford over his shoulder. "Your
parables are as usual beyond my comprehension."

" 'Tis your own fault, seein' you've no imagination.
You'd never do fur a poet. Well thin, you must
know that that ould gintl'man av a monkey widout
a tail owns three parts av the village. He lends
out the proceeds av his snake-shkin medicines an'
cat's-liver pills at Simple Interest,—one yen, one
sen,—which has tu be paid punctually at sunset,
otherwise it's Compound. This just means 365 per
cent. per annum, as you'll see fur yersilf, since as I
said before you were brought up on the Multiplication table, saysoned wid the Westminster
Shorter Catechism. Well, he just has the whole
colliction av thim frightened tu call their sowls,
much less the fish they catch, their own. For
you'll see him now a-prowlin' down at the boats,
like a ghoul or a hob-goblin, pickin' an' choosin'
and summarily annixin' the best they've tuk from
the say. An' he has it all at his own price, which
is nixt tu no price at all, an' thin he loads up that
steamer wid it, an' sinds it tu Tokyo where he sells
it fur the best price in the market. So he owns

three parts av the village, body an' sowl, an' all the
houses av pleasure beyant on the rise, an' a crowd
av villas on the bluff,—that cottage you were playin'
Peepin' Tom at among thim. An' his son is a
lawyer who helps him tu chate the executioner.
He cultivates a mustache, wears European continuations an' a pot hat, an' is the victim av Parlia-
mintry aspirations. It's said's he's tryin' tu get
hould av the gurl forninst,"—he nodded over
toward the cliffs on the other side —"bekaz she
knows English, an' would make a wife to shew off
an' be proud av when he goes tu Ameriky as
Ambassador."

"That's rather a tall programme isn't it?"

" Tall ! Shure, it's just loike thim. There isn't a Japanese among thim but has enough consate tu think himself a fit and proper maan tu ascind to the Great White Throne itsilf wid cridentials and an ultimatum if he gets the chance. But what about thim wather-colours ? Let's hav a luk at art as expounded by Gifford. Is this the picture ye've made av it ? "

He leant over and took up the sketch he had treated so despitefully as a beginning to his day's work.

He held it first to one side and then to the other, and looked at it with the air of a Hebrew picture-dealer inspecting the efforts of genius without heels to its boots, and bent on buying cheap. The inspection began in disapproval and ended in disgust.

"An' ye call *this* a piece av art do yez? ' *View av Misaki wid Japanese childer at play* ' Well, all I can say, it's lucky ye've tould in so many wurruds pwhat it was meant fur! It's a moighty queer and riposeful notion av play that thim childer seem tu have! And yer perverted taste in selectin' thim ould-toime cumberers av the say as fit subjects to hand down to immortality! It's niver a change they've made in thim since the days av ould Will Adams in spite av all his tachin' and prachin' an bein' made into a

sort av Shinto god an' havin' stone lanterns put up
fur his ghost to see by.   An' it's wan sign av
enlightenment an conversion tu Christian principles
that the Japanese Governmint are thryin tu improve
thim off the face av the wathers."

"What is wrong with them?"

"Wrong wid thim! What was wrong wid your
Japanese models? Everything! In the first place
every maan av the crew mistakes himself fur
captain. An' pwhat can you do wid only wan
single square sail? Nothing but run wid the
wind. As a work av art yer picture is con-
timptible."

"What improvements would you suggest?" asked Gifford drily.

"Blot it all out, an' do it over agin, an' moind
above all things to put a dacent craft into it!"

"And where is that to be found?"

"Well now, that's pwhat I call insolince worthy
av tin hours pack-dhrill. Shure an' isn't it the
Komachi that's lying afore yez?"

"And do ye honestly think, ye red-wud Irishman, that abeelity to limn your tub of a cockle-shell
is the sole title to get hung—in the Academy I
mean. You're worse than Koto san, your *sendo*,—
that creature wi' the manners and notions, the vices
and virtues of a Newfoundland dog. His only
criterion of intelligence, to say nothing of genius
is the style in which a man handles the *Komachi's*
tiller. He'd call the Prime Minister of Japan himself a *baka* (fool) and no statesman if he ———
But what do you say to this? Surely this will
please you!" broke off the artist impatiently.

Gifford picked another sketch out from his case
and handed it over. O'Rafferty's eyes lighted up.
He heaved a great sigh of satisfaction.

"Faith, me son!" he said approvingly, "It's the
elemints av immortal gaynius ye've contrived to put
into it this toime. This wather-colour av yours is just
a jewel av an etching, wid the clouds all so nat'ral
loike and a goulden flood av moonlight shtramin'

out from behoind thim from some pint that remanes tu be determined,—just like a problem in
Todhunter's Euclid or in the Geometry av Co-
ordinates. An' thim Japanese junks wid their screw-
necks av masts make a first-class piece av local
colouring, they being true tu nature, a foine adorn-
mint tu the landscape, and things av beauty loikely
tu prove joys for ever. But it's the *Komachi* that
makes the picture what it is, an' it's only justice
ye've rindered her, though there was no call fur yez
tu limn the dingy in the risimblance av a big black
beetle that's mistuk his up-side fur his down. Yes,
me frind, there's hope fur yez in Israel afther all;
if you only could always have a maan at your
elbow, wid thrue artistic taste loike mesilf."

"To exercise me in drawing tubs like the
Komachi?"

The ironical tone of this suggestion brought a
shower of vituperation and a Japanese pillow
upon Gifford's head. Just then breakfast was
announced and this interfered with reprisals.

IV.

"Now thin," said O'Raff, after the omelettes had all disappeared as he produced the everlasting pipe. "It's a glorious day we're to have av it. The wind——"

"Oh! Confound the wind!" interrupted Gifford impatiently. "Do you fancy I am going out with you again to enjoy the pleasure of having the nether parts of me all roasted on that frying-pan of a deck of yours? Not if I know it!"

" Musha! now thin, just hould yer whisht! It's round to Kamakura I'm goin' tu run yez tu let you finish off the champion bull-god av Japaan. Ye haven't done the Dai-butsu yet an' every globe-trotter is supposed to know all about him, even to the diminsions av his thumb an' the number av the curls av his hair. It's eight hundred an' thirty there are av thim. So get on board wid yez, an obey orders!"

Gifford muttered a lurid protest, but he allowed himself to be persuaded. They went down to get on board, but the dingy had disappeared.

"That young divil av a Santaro has stolen her!" commented O'Rafferty. " But more power tu his elbow! It's a foine man he'll grow up to be yet, wid all his fondness for the ocean an' the things thereof. Musha, but it's a foine wind to take us round we'll have."

They were soon out of the harbour and round the point with a rousing breeze whistling astern of them as they stood on across the bay. O'Rafferty, of course, was at the tiller with his pipe in his mouth and enough smoke flowing therefrom to excuse the uninitiated land-lubber for mistaking the *Komachi* for an auxiliary screw.

" Halloo, there's the *botchan* navigatin' his craft as bould as Columbus!" the Irishman said, with a shoreward wave of his disengaged hand. " It's a

picnic on oysters an' shell-fish he clearly manes tu have, wid wan av thim twelve feet cryabs thrown in by way av desert tu wash thim down wid."

An hour served to run them across the reach to the beach in front of the cradle of Japanese feudalism.

"Av course," said O'Rafferty as they struggled over the loose sand on to the rice-fields, "ye know that wanst this was a city av a million souls. An' now it's peopled by nothing but ghosts an' smells that you can't understand. The guide-book says it was as good as Kilkenny, being the scene av innumerable contests between rival factions, and av many bloody deeds. It wanted none av the climints av civilisation unless it were newspapers and sixteen-button boots fur the wimmen-folks. it had its faymale lady collictors, fur we're tould wan of the ladies of Yoritomo's Court undertook to gather funds for the eriction av Dai-butsu. An' by the token, here we are in front av that stupenjus haythen monument. Listen tu the wurruds av Instruction, me son."

He stopped in his tracks and opening his *Murray* began to declaim, sawing the air with his left hand all the time :—

"*The Daibutsu, or ' Great Buddha,' stands alone among Japanese works of art. No other gives such an impression of majesty, or so truly symbolises the* central idea of Buddhism—the intellectual calm which comes of perfected knowledge and the subjugation of all passion. But to be fully appreciated, the Daibutsu must be visited many times."

"Well now, no doubt thim were the sintimints av the tidal wave that twice ran away wid his house. But let us purceed wid the argyment."

He again took up his parable, this time shouting at the top of his voice :—

"The Dai-butsu is best seen from about half way up the approach. Its dimensions are approximately as follows :—

Height—49 ft. 7 in.

"Oh! bother you!" said Gifford, striking the book from his hand. "I don't want to hear a pilfered sermon. Give us some original facts of your own. If they aren't handy, you'll manufacture them I know. It's a way of yours!"

"Facts is it ye call fur? I scorn thim; it's only truth I'll tell yez. His bump av wisdom is 9 in. high, and it's bigger than the wan they raised on Paddy Maclure wid a shillelagh at the wake av his mother-in-law. An' his face is 8 ft. 5 in. in length, which is long enough fur a professional undertaker or a Methody lay-pracher widout the extra inches. An' if yez make bould to vinture widin his entrails, ye'll find that his bowels av compassion have

fur their principal ingradients, emptiness, adver-
tisements of curio stores and quack medicines,
an' a foine colliction av the autographs av folks
noted only fur baad taste an' worse than faymale
vanity. It was in 1612 that Saris's men first set
the example tu scribblin' globe-trotters in that respect. They were the first sample of "'Arry" in
Japan, fur ould Will Adams was a gintleman an'
wouldn't disgrace himself by lavin' any such a con-
timptible ricord av insignificance behoind him."

"Well, that may be so, but I don't want a lecture
on ethics and manners,—at least from Mr. Phelan
O'Rafferty," put in Gifford, making preparations for
work. "What else have you to say about him?"

"Only that he's a foine ould specimen av a bull-
god; bull-gods bein' wan av the only three great
things they have in this consated Land av Lilli-
put."

"Explain!" grunted Gifford as he went on mix-
ing his colours.

"Explain, is it? Well, thin, you must know that
thim folks call their counthry Dai Nippon. Dai
Nippon,—Great Japan! Great Japan! Shure it's not
much bigger than a wan cow's feed in Clonmel,
an' it's only three great things they have in it. An'
thim three are haythen bull-gods an' cryabs and
unholy perverters av veracity!"

"That latter may be so, Phelan, ma friend; but

these folks are some function of the truth after all, and that's more than your imagination is when it is its day out, as it seems to be on this occasion," responded the artist taking up his brush.

"Get out wid yez! It's mesilf that scorns yer company. Take care av yerself till I come back."

O'Rafferty walked off with his nose in the air and disappeared in the street of the village. Half an hour later Gifford noticed a whitish cloud of tobacco smoke upcurling from the summit of Inamura-ga-saki. O'Rafferty was enjoying the landscape from there.

When he descended some few hours later on, it was time to think of returning. They got on board and hoisted sail for home. Just as they were approaching the end of the long neck of land that terminates in Cape Misaki they were startled by a cry of fear and distress. They both sprang up and looked shorewards.

"It's the boy attacked by a monster of some kind; a shark seemingly!" said Gifford.

"Shark be blowed!" interrupted O'Rafferty excitedly. "As if a shark ever took to walkin' abroad over dhry land. It's more a cryab beloike. An' by the Holy Moses! a cryab it is, an a divil av a baste at that! What are ye doin'? Wait till I bring yez in another hundred yards!"

The last sentence had reference to the action
Gifford was taking. He had divested himself of
his coat and shoes and was on the point of diving
overboard.

"Now thin, more power to yer arm!" shouted
O'Rafferty as in response to another shriek of pain
and terror Gifford sprang into the deep. A few
strokes brought his feet in touch with land; he
rushed forward driving the water in showers before
him. He reached the shore not one second too
soon.

By stay-at-home wise-acres who fondly fancy their
experience to be the final test of reality you would
be set down as a romancer if you ventured to speak
of such a thing as a ten-foot crab. Yet you might
stretch the span of the *Inachus Kempferi* as given
in the Encyclopedia Britannica a stray cubit or two
without tampering unduly with the elasticity of
veracity. Specimens of these monsters have been
found with a stretch of fifteen feet between the tips
of the two great toes when outspread. The body
itself is comparatively insignificant,—not much more
than a foot in diameter. As O'Rafferty put it 'the
craythur was lanky enough fur a Corn-shtalk, with
lots av legs all long an' slinder enough fur a shpoi-
der.' These crustacea are usually found at the
Bonin Islands, and occasionally at Enoshima, and
in these two spots only. This one had somehow or

other found its way across the bay to Misaki. And
when it had wheeled round to return to its habitat
it had found its way barred by Santaro.

As Gifford rushed forward with the oar he seized
from the dingy, the creature had raised itself on its
legs and lifting one of its great toes aloft had
brought it down upon Santaro with force enough
to upset him. Luckily it was not the toe itself but
the thin part of the joint behind it that struck his
shoulder. The creature had just grabbed him by
the thigh when Gifford fell upon it with the oar and
shore off three of its spider-like supports with a
lusty stroke. With a squeal of rage and pain that
was a good deal more than uncanny it swung round
to meet him as if on a swivel. What a horribly
fiendish look there was in its little round bead-like
eyes! Gifford was ready for it before it could do
any mischief; he brought the oar down right on
its body and it cracked as if it had been an egg-
shell. Then he pounded it till it was nothing but
fragments. He turned and picked up Santaro and
carried him off to the *Komachi*, to an accompaniment
of loud-voiced Hibernian expressions of approval.

V.

The youngster had met with a serious mauling. His left shoulder was badly mangled and contused, while his thigh also shewed nasty wounds. When they got him on board, Gifford set to work to wash them and tie them up as best he could. As he was finishing his surgery the boy went off into a faint.

"It's a moighty foine doctor ye are!" commented O'Rafferty. "Ye seem tu be as powerful as chloroform. At the same toime, ye were helpful to a degree when you tied together the tatters av me right calf afther McNeil's zareba. You remimber that toime?

"Yes, I have a faint recollection if it."

"Faint recollection? Is that all? There I was wid a horse atop av me, an' a brute av a nigger wid

the misguided curiosity av a vivisectionist wantin'
badly tu explore me inward parts wid the business
end av his spear! If't hadn't been for you, now, old
man,—— Shake!"

O'Rafferty abruptly broke off and held out a
great hairy paw. Gifford accepted it with some
hesitation; he knew what O'Rafferty didn't, and
that was the strength of the latter when under the
influence of a generous emotion or of whiskey.

By this time they had rounded the spit and made
the harbour. The *Komachi* was brought to, some
hundred yards short of her usual anchorage.

"Now, thin," said O'Rafferty, "the remainder
av this job is *my* wurruk, I take it. An' it's a tall
story I'll tell av your pluck, altho' it's no mean
foundation av truth the airy fabric av me imagination will rist upon."

"Oh! come now, it's really too kind of you.
But I could never think of giving you all the bother.
Besides you'll want to see after the *Komachi*," put
in Gifford hurriedly.

"Now, botheration! It's a lot av throuble, isn't
it? You've done your share av the wurruk
an' now I'll do mine. It's Homer ricordin' the
praises av Ash-heels as Brit Harte makes what-
dye-call him misname him."

"I couldn't think of allowing such a thing for a
moment. Your colours would be too flaming, and

I'd feel as if I were blushing all over. I'll go myself.'"

"But you can't spake tin wurruds av the lingo! How cud *you* explain? They'd kill ye fur murtherin' the *botchan*, if ye tuk him back as he is, widout bein' able tu tell how he came by the marks av his clapper-clawin'!"

"Oh, never mind; I couldn't think of bothering you. I'll take my chance. Besides the youngster will speak for himself."

By this time the artist had caught Santaro up in his arms. In spite of all O'Rafferty's eloquence he stepped into the dingy, and told Koto to give way. He sprang ashore, and carrying the boy with all the tenderness 'av a father' as the critic he left behind him observed, he passed through the streets with a great crowd gathering behind in his wake, and up the steep flights of temple-steps and disappeared within the gateway of the villa that opened to receive him.

O'Rafferty scratched his head to aid the movement of his thinking machinery. For some time his face was as blank as the door of a church with nothing beyond Inland Revenue notices to adorn it. At last a gleam of intelligence flashed into his eyes and rippled all over his countenance.

"I parceave!" he remarked, cocking his left optic knowingly with a sardonic grin. "It's an ould

campaigner in the fields av iniquity that maan
Gifford is! I remimber him in Cairo. It's now six
o'clock.—if I see him by sundown I'll not be disappointed. An' I'll dine alone by mesilf this
evenin', fur if I wait fur him it's could meat the
roast chicken 'ull be."

Whereupon O'Raff returned solitary to the re-
treat. He ordered dinner, and then took up the
binocular to rake the villa vis-à-vis. But as he remarked *sotto voce*, the task was 'shuparfluous.'
Not a vestige of its inmates were to be seen.

"The cunnin' divil!" he muttered. "It's not
till mornin' I'll see him."

VI.

It was really late when Gifford returned; the
light-house was already blinking and winking over
the sea where darkness sat brooding in heavy silence.
The only sounds to be heard were the ticking of the
cheap eight-day clock in the alcove and the grunting
of a steamer inward bound. O'Rafferty had already
thrown himself down on his quilt and was breathing
the measured breath of one sleeping the sleep of
the just. He turned over on his side as Gifford
entered, and began to mumble and misquote :—

> " *The ox toils through the furrow*
> *Obedient tu the goad ;*
> *The patient ass, up t.mple-steps*
> *Plods wid his weary load,*
> *An' Venus luves the whishpers*
> *Av ploighted youth and maid*
> *In Misaki's summer starloight——*

Arrah! ye spalpeen, ye've dislocated the remanes av me only survoivin' ancle."

This lapse from poetry into plain but forcible prose was doubtless occasioned by the vigorous wrench the artist gave the foot he laid hold of. For it should be explained that O'Rafferty was tender as to his understandings. At El Teb a shell had burst unduly close to him and had carried away a part of the bone of the left shin, besides sticking him pretty well full of pebbles all over his body. But O'Rafferty got well soon enough to take a hand in the solemn interment of his dismembered fragment. And to this day the 'wake' that preceded the funeral of his left tibia, is more than a memory in his old regiment. For the sayings and doings and eke the drinking on that occasion were passing wonderful.

"Well, now, me valiant conqueror av cryabs," proceeded O'Rafferty without getting up, "it's all very well tu be loively an' gay, but will ye be ready tu start at three i'the mornin'?"

"I say, old man, couldn't we put in four or five more days here?" began Gifford hesitatingly, as he seated himself on the edge of the verandah and set about unlacing his boots.

"Phwilat!" almost shrieked O'Rafferty, jumping up in wrath and amazement at the mere mention of the idea. 'Do yez know phwhat ye're askin'?

It's wurruse than requistin' a pore lone widdey
whose only consolation is religion tu shtay
away from Mass av a Sunday! Ow! Ye haythen! Don't yez know that to-morrow is the sailin'
race an' that the *Komachi* so far has crossed the
loine first every toime, an' that wid fair play she's
tu annix all the plates an' prizes av the year! And
thin, phwat about the *China* on Monday?"

"Well, that's just it!" said Gifford shifting uneasily. "You see, I think I'll stay another week
and go by the *Parthia*. It's quicker and less
fatiguing by that route, and I'll be in New York
sooner than if I started on Monday. You see, time
is a matter of importance."

"It is, me son, no doubt! But fur pwhat purpose
and at which ind,—here or beyant?"

"And besides I saw a bit of landscape to-night
I should like to do before I go."

"Bit av landscape! A small but purty wan,
I'll be sworn,—a square fut or two av shkin!'"

"And furthermore I have found a man that can
teach me something. That fine old gentleman
over on the bluff there can put me up to a thing or
two, I've just discovered."

"Indade! It's moighty modest ye've waxed all
av a suddint! Haven't yez as good as tould me
till the dhrums av me ears could stand it no longer
that there wasn't a man in Japaan yez could learn

anything from in your own line? 'In landscape they've no prospective and in figures they're purely convintional.' That's the way it ran, me son, till two seconds ago."

"Well, but I've just seen reason to amend my opinion. That old gentleman is a man of notions, and I misdoubt not he can be induced to part with some of them."

"Fur your benefit av course!" put in O'Rafferty ironically.

"Yes, for my benefit, of course!"

"And ye're sure tu take in all he sez,—ivvery syllabub?" This was uttered very slowly and in the driest of dry tones.

"I hope so," replied the artist submissively.

"Maan, I thought yez had become modest, but it's worse than a home-grown Japanese in yer consate I find yez. Ye're tu take lessons in art,—in immortal art, from a Japanese painter maan who's as guiltless av the Widdey's English as I am av Hebrew, an' all the Nihongo you know is scantier than the clothes a coolie wears tu consale his summer nakedness wid. Ow! but it's a bad counthry is Japan fur a maan bumptious by nature! Consate's in the very atmosphere av the land, an' me pore friend, ye'd seem tu have caught it mortal hard. An' it's worse than a ten-horse power malaria!"

To this Gifford vouchsafed no reply. He went

on unlacing his boots, tugging furiously at the strings. O'Rafferty paused for a minute and then went on :—

"Faith, thin, it's meself that admires your strathegy. In the first place ye make frinds wid the ould maan all along av yer drawin' an' daubin'. An' av course you knowin' nothing about Japanese, and he half as much av English, there's no need av Phelan O'Rafferty as a medium fur the advancement av international intercourse. Ye don't want any wan tu translate his instructions, bekaz, bein' a nat'ral born-jaynius, wurruds will be shuparfluous."

The air seemed to quiver with the irony wherewith O'Rafferty was lashing the devoted Gifford.

"But yez want me tu give up me very sowl's mate an 'dhrink, just bekaz ye've tuk a fancy tu a bit av landscape, an' bekaz ye've suddenly found that toime is valuable, and bekaz ye've all at wanst discovered that the soonest way to get to New York is to delay here fur a week, an' bekaz ye've found an ould gintl'man of whose lingo ye can just spake foive wurruds besides *doko* (where), and *ikura* (how much), tu put the finishing touches to yer artistic eddication. An' in the midst av it all, ye think Mr. O'Rafferty has suddenly parted wid all his common sense!"

"Well, then you positively won't stay?"

"Stay! Do you think it loikely? No, I'll tell

yez though! I'll go miself all alone, an' I'll lave
you here to paint that bit av landscape, an' tu get
tu Ameriky quicker, an' to get that gintl'man whose
tongue ye spake so glibly tu finish ye off like a
young lady at a boardin'-school. An' I'll come back
wid the *Komachi* tu fetch yez this day week, an' if
you get into mischief whin I'm not by to purtect
yez, shure an' it's mesilf that ain't the risponsible
party. Come off the tiles and get to bed wid you
an' let a dacent maan sleep!"

And forthwith O'Rafferty threw himself on his
back and relapsed into silence and slumber.

When Gifford awoke the following morning he
found himself alone, and the *Komachi* gone from
her anchorage.

VII.

It was late next morning when Gifford awoke
with a yawn and stretched his arms above his head.
And wonderful were the arms he stretched out;
long and clean and sinewy and powerful.   They
were in keeping with the rest of his physique, lithe
and limber, but at the same time firm withal and
hard as the finest steel that ever went on the edge
of a Massamune blade.   He paused for a moment
to collect himself and then he sprang nimbly off his
quilt.

As he proceeded to dress he went on whistling gently.   This was not by any means for
want of thought.   For Gifford, although usually a
man of Spartan-like brevity, had a thinking-machine

of a very high power, and usually had it a-working.
But a person might be in his company for some
considerable time without having any notion of the
fact. He was not addicted to making display of
his mental garnishings unless with some very
good and substantial reason for so doing. In
war-time, he reasoned, cartridges were served
out to kill, and in the battle of life good talk was
too telling and precious to be recklessly spent for
naught. Wherefore he was careful to keep a tight
curb upon his tongue, as a rule merely uttering
himself sufficiently to induce other people to de-
liver themselves for his benefit. When he got
among the ordinary ruck of so-called society, seek-
ing with its factitious chatter to hide its insipid
shallowness, it was his wont to assume the rôle of
a dullard. For that tended to throw people off
their guard in his presence and gave him better
opportunities of reading the pages of the book of
human life, and that was his favourite volume.
But when he did run across any one who really
had ideas, he both could and did talk; conversation
in that case being good for the soul, and a moral
and intellectual duty incumbent on him in accordance with his scheme of existence.

That scheme of existence of his was at once
simple, comprehensive and practical, but he kept
it to himself. He did not go round proclaiming

it from the house-tops in the fashion of the man
with a mission. In truth he was the reverse of a
man who made a business of asserting either his be-
liefs or himself,—that is where trifles only were
involved. For example, for the last three months
ever since the day they had met on Yokohama *hatoba*, he had seemingly allowed himself to be
dominated and ingloriously henpecked by what in
his heart of hearts he characterised as 'that amia-
ble gas-pot O'Rafferty.' Yet no one knew better
than O'Rafferty himself that that sort of thing had
its limits. When Gifford once chose to put his foot
down and to make a stand over anything, it was about
as easy to divert him from the tenor of his way as
for faith to move mountains. Wherefore when he
diplomatically gave his friend to understand that he
meant to stay for an extra week at Misaki, O'Rafferty
never for a moment thought seriously of arguing
the point. Without more ado, as he phrased it
himself, he just 'gave the baste his head,' fully alive
to the fact that when it came to piecing together a
long series of delicate and intricate details necessary for the attainment of any given object the head
in question was a rare good one.

"The cunnin' divil!" the Irishman muttered to
himself, looking up at the bungalow as next morning at cock-crow the *Komachi* swept out round the
light-house point. "He's slapin' as innocint-loike

as a sivin years infant. An' it's the craft av ould
Nick he has. Frobisher av the Ligation, an' Wilson
av the Dipartment av Justice, an' Somerville the
big Yokohama merchant are just moiles astern in
the race, although they started wid toime allowance
an' everything else in their favour. The divil
clearly enough made up his moind whin he saw the
gurl, an' Providence was foolish enough tu give
him a hoist ahead in the mather av that cryab."

It was four hours thereafter when Gifford awoke.
As he leisurely disposed of breakfast, he reviewed
the occurrences of yesterday. And the result he
arrived at was on a par with the judgment of the
protagonist in the drama of the creation when he
contemplated the outcomes of his handiwork. They
were all very good,—for his purpose.

First of all there was his entrance though the
surging crowd that with much pattering of *geta*
thronged the door-way of the court-yard of the old
painter's abode. Then when the wicket clicked
behind him and his burden, he passed through a
gate in the hedge to the left and found a fairy
paradise around him. Here and there great old
gnarled pines with huge trunks and limbs all twisted
and knotted into contortions like the muscles of
Japanese wrestlers as limned in theatre posters.
Under the shade of their whispering boughs an
expanse of turf, dotted with little knolls; among

them of course the never-failing miniature of the
eternal Peerless Mountain.   Then impossible looking dwarf-pines that had reached a stature of six
inches in sixty years, wonderful palms and plants
in still more wonderful pots, walks laid with flag-
stones never meant to be contaminated by shoe-
leather, and bridgelets and pools and fish-ponds
with great sleepy gaudily-coloured *koi* occasionally
energetic enough to stir the waters into ripples with
a lazy flop of their cumbrous tails.

All this the artist's quick eye took in at a glance. He advanced over the paving-stones to the open verandah; for it was in the garden of the house he now was, and that in the household economy of this land of topsy-turveydom occupies the position of the back-yard in Anglo-Saxon countries. When he turned to the right he had left behind him the *genka* or front-door, with its little sliding wicket, to enter at which you have to double yourself up like a camp-stool. This he had done to save delay. He went forward and gently laid Santaro on the *tatami* (mats) and then rapped on the boards.

As he waited for an answer he glanced round the interior. It was charming in its artistic yet chaste simplicity. The mats were spotlessly white, and

seemed to breathe out coolness upon the sweltering afternoon. The only furnishings upon them were a fireless *hibachi* (brazier), a tobacco-box, with its fire-jar and bamboo ash-box, a set of Hizen tea-ware, a chequer-board near the verandah, and one with its two pots of white and black stones atop of it, placed against the far pillar of the *toko-no-ma* (alcove). The pillars of this alcove were wonderful samples of that kind of wood-work in which the Japanese so excel. In accordance with national ideas, its only ornament was a flower vase also from the potteries of Arita, with a dwarf-orange tree in it, while another occupied the small side-alcove beside the closely-ribbed paper-window.

He had barely time to take this in before he heard an almost inaudible footstep and the sweep of a dress in the passage beyond. The *karakami* was slid back an inch or two, a pair of lustrous eyes in the sweetest of faces glanced wonderingly into the room, and then the slide was pushed back again with a hurried click.

Eager voices were audible in rapid talk in the *rōka* (passage) beyond and then came a heavier footstep, and an old gentleman entered the room and came gravely forward to where Gifford sat on the edge of the verandah. He squatted down on the floor, and with an anxious and inquiring glance at the still unconscious Santaro he bowed to the ground, very politely but at the same time very coldly. For he was by no means fond of foreign faces. He then said something, which of course Gifford could not understand, but which he rightly assumed to be the Japanese equivalent for 'What can I do for you?'

The artist by way of an answer merely lifted the clothes from Santaro's shoulder and showed the blood-stained bandage. The old man started slightly in spite of himself. His look plainly demanded an explanation.

Gifford was ready with one in a trice. He whipped out his note-book and his pencil and with a few deft strokes limned Santaro in the claws of the crab. His crabship would not have been flattered with his portrait; it was the most villainous and sinful-looking monster that could be met with out of a nightmare. Gifford presented this to view, and then he quickly worked in the outline of his own part in the piece.

"*Ha! Ha! Hei! Hei!*" exclaimed the old gentleman in wonderment. "*Naruhodo!*" And he started up and turned to Santaro, and then again to the picture and its limner. He looked at the latter with keen interest. Just then Santaro uttered a heavy sigh, and opened his eyes.

"*Kani! Kani!* (Crab! Crab!)" he said, looking round in a dazed, frightened fashion.

The grandfather again turned to him, this time
with reassuring and comforting words. The youngster soon struggled into a sitting position. The
old man shewed him the picture, and then the boy
began to pour out a long torrent of explanation, in
which there were many *domos*, answered by antiphonal *domos* and *naruhodos* from his startled auditor.
At the conclusion of the recital the grandfather
turned round with a flushed face to Gifford, and
bending forward till his face almost touched the
mats, he uttered himself in a long flow of un-
understandable eloquence. In this prostration there
was nothing servile or mean even to the artist's
censorious eyes; the whole thing was characterized
by a simple dignity that carried with it a something
of pride. Gifford judged it was thanks he was re-
ceiving, so he also bent forward on his hands, and
by smiles and head-shakes tried to convey that
what he had done was a trifle, and that any one
else under the circumstances, etc. etc. etc.,—in
short all the Anglo-Saxon common-places appropriate to the occasion.

But the old gentleman was not contented to let
the matter rest there. He started up and clapped
his hands, calling out something that sounded like
Ayame. His call was immediately answered; a
karakami was thrust aside, and a new character
appeared on the scene.

VIII.

It was the face that had first greeted Gifford's
rap on the verandah. She came into the room
with shy and modest grace, and advancing with
her long robe sweeping the floor, and the
tiniest of tabied feet peeping out and in from
its folds, she bowed herself on the floor before
her uncle and Gifford, and then sat up with
hands folded on her lap awaiting instructions.
Gifford without staring offensively, yet took her
in with all his eyes. There was an indefinable
charm about her,—about her face, her hair, the
fashion of her dress and the way she carried it,
her poise, and her manner that in spite of himself
sent his heart a-beating and the blood coursing
through him with a rush.

Her uncle talked to her with many *o*'s and *go*'s
and *masu*'s, evidently with Gifford as the main
subject of his sentences and periods. At last he
stopped and made another obeisance to the artist.

Then the girl turned towards him with what he
thought the sweetest smile he had ever seen.

"My uncle," she began, "bids me say thanks
to you,—very many true thanks. Your great kindness he will never forget. And henceforward he
begs you to honour his unworthy side with your
friendship. Excuse me, because I speak the English language very unskillfully."

She uttered the words slowly and with evident
effort, accentuating every one of them with the
utmost clearness and distinctness. Her voice was
soft and low, with a sweetness in its tones that
Gifford knew would be unto him even as a lasting
memory. As she spoke she raised her eyes,—and
wonderful those eyes with their long dark lashes
were, and looked him in the face, calmly and
quietly and simply. Man of the world as he was,
at first he almost felt at a loss how to answer.
He merely contented himself with the usual
formulæ of such an occasion. But he was careful
not to place either her or himself on a level with a
tea-house girl by launching into compliments on
her linguistic ability.

The old gentleman then turned himself to her and

uttered himself at length. The girl listened atten-
tively, occasionally putting in a '*Hei!*' '*Hei!*' of
wonder, or a remark in an interrogative tone, with
quick looks of concern at Santaro who was watching
the scene intently all the while, and then again she
addressed herself to Gifford.

"My uncle says *that* Santaro has told him so much,
and that you have very skilfully drawn a picture
about the struggle, but please, will you tell him full
particulars of the matter?"

She said this with slightly more animation than
before, Gifford fancied. He immediately complied
with her request and told simply and directly and
concisely how the thing had happened. Her interest
grew as he proceeded; she kept on interpreting to
her uncle, occasionally questioning Gifford with
waxing keenness.

In the course of his explanation the old man
handed her Gifford's sketch. She looked at it
closely.

"My uncle says *that* you are really an artist!"
she said in a tone that was as much a question as
an assertion.

Gifford modestly admitted that he had been
brought up to use the brush and the pencil, and said
that was the way he made his living. With a swift
turn of her head she communicated the fact to her
uncle.

"*So desu ka?*" exclaimed the old man in tones
of genuine pleasure.

His face lit up with a great light of sympathy, and
bowing once more on his forehead, he sat up and
spoke hurriedly and eagerly to the girl.

" He says *that*,—' As for you it is much honour
you do by giving him your friendship and because
you have so kindly called upon him to-day. As for
you, henceforth he hopes very often for the pleasure
of your company. He says *that*.' "

She placed a strongish accent upon 'that,' as
Japanese do upon the particle '*to*,' which ushers in
and winds up indirect speech in their tongue. She
was evidently thinking in Japanese and translating.

Then scarcely waiting for a reply she clapped
her hands. Gifford noticed what dainty little hands
they were, with long taper fingers and pink nails.

" Excuse our rudeness," she went on. " Will
you be pleased to partake of our imperfect hospitality ? Some tea and cakes ?"

Gifford said he would be delighted. He watched
her closely as she set the refreshments before him,
and addressed herself to the tea-making.

In a few minutes he was offered a dainty cup
of real Uji tea between which and the tannic-acid
slops manufactured by pouring luke-warm water
over tea-sweepings such as are usually served up
with intent to do serious bodily injury in wayside

inns and *chaya* (tea-houses) there is a great gulf
fixed.

As he sipped it, she began to ply him with her
uncle's questions; "What was his nationality?
When had he come to Japan? What did he think
of Japanese artists' work?"

He took the opportunity the last query offered
to say he would like to see some of Mr. Tanaka's,
—that was the old gentleman's name.

This request was taken as a high compliment
and immediately complied with. Tanaka san was
delighted. It was a revelation to him to find that
one of the suspected foreigners could so enter into
the spirit of his conceptions. More than one hour
winged its flight at this occupation and then Gifford
all unwillingly arose to take his leave. He needed
no pressing to promise that next day he would
return and bring some of his own productions for
his host's inspection. Then as he rose and said
good-bye, Ayame had asked him how long he was
to stay in Japan. His heart gave a leap as he
marked the clouding of her face and the dimming
of her eyes when he answered one week more.
Tanaka san insisted on seeing him to the gate, and
on escorting him some distance on his homeward
way.

IX.

All this Gifford went over in his mind as he slowly fixed his easel for work.

He placed it in position and made everything ready with unusual care. Then he began and went ahead with all his soul in his fingers. Four long hours he toiled on without intermission and then he stopped for luncheon. As he sat down he looked at his handiwork severely. His brows came down in a frown. He did not sing Jacobite songs in a joyful strain on this forenoon. He dashed up and drove his clenched fist through his canvas with something that sounded like an imprecation.

"That Ayame!" he muttered, "That daub! You're supposed to make strong work by idealising the real ; this time it seems as if I had tried to reverse the process, and made a complete mess of it con-se-quent-ly. And they tell me I'm an artist! Oh! Lord!"

The wind-up of his soliloquy was a moan of despair as he measured the gap beteen his conception and his execution. However not much else could be expected when he took to *chiqueing* his work.

He sat down with a sigh and appealed to his pipe for consolation. He remained for the best part of half-an-hour with one leg crossed over the other, looking out across the harbour and up at the cliff beyond. But his gaze seemed to travel further than the cliff; he evidently had his thinking-cap on.

" Yes," he muttered to himself at last. " I fancy it can *just* be done. But at the same time it seems a burning shame to do it. But, good Heavens! What a chance! I've never had the like of it in my life. Anyhow we'll see what we'll see. Sufficient unto the day, κ.τ.λ., as they write in the foot-notes to Greek plays."

He got up and fossicked out a port-folio from the chaotic welter his traps made on the floor. He opened it and turned over sketch after sketch.

" I daresay this will do!" he said to himself. " There's variety enough here, I should fancy, and material sufficient to lead up to the casting of the hook, wherewith I count upon landing my fish."

He turned the key in the lock and put the portfolio under his arm. Then he fared forth down the sandy path, across the water in the crazy ferry-boat with its load of painfully polite passengers, through the streets of the village with their smells ancient and fish-like and up the flights of temple steps. As he passed the houses of pleasure on the upper slopes, the girls ogled him and made a vain pretence of blushing, but like that model young fool in Excelsior he gave no heed to their invitation to ' Deign to do an honourable exit this way,' which as might naturally be expected in this land of *saka-sama* (upside-down) stands for ' Come in please.' In one of these places he caught a glimpse of the droop of a set of European coat-tails. On looking closer he discerned a Japanese in frock-coat, white waist-coat, and occidental continuations, with rings, chains and a waxed moustache, being ministered to by three buxom and blooming Hebes. The un-failing pot-hat lay beside him on the floor. His features were not prepossessing. The forehead was low, while a pair of shifty fish-like eyes seemed to look out with everlasting morbid suspicion over abnormally high sallow cheeks and the stump. of a snub nose with the curve of the roof of a Buddhist temple. These eyes met Gifford's as he passed, and immediately they dropped and made for cover like the fox when he sniffs the hounds.

When the artist reached the villa, he found a visitor already in possession of the floor. It was the old Chinese doctor from below.

"Most likely rent collecting," thought Gifford to himself.

He rose as Gifford entered, and took his departure with many humble bows, yet with a look on his smirking face that filled the painter with a powerful but unholy desire to seize him forcibly by the *obi* and the neck of his *yukata* and run him gently out through the gate and some little way down the temple-steps. He looked for all the world like O'Rafferty's description of him,—' an ould wizened pithecoid av a 365 per cent. blood-sucker av a baboon.'

Tanaka san's temper had evidently been ruffled, although it needed a tolerably acute observer to note the fact. Gifford however had already acquired sufficient acquaintance with Japanese forms and manners to be able to read between the lines in this instance. He caught the glimmer of a fitful spark of anger flickering in the depths of the old man's eyes. He also caught sight of a box in the passage beyond containing something like sword-sheaths in yellow *furoshiki* (cloth-wrappers). It was hid from view when the *karakami* clicked together as he entered and made his obeisance.

Gifford after the usual tedious formality of salutation, took up his portfolio and unlocked it. As he began to take out his sketches the old man clapped his hands, and Ayame answered his call. Her response to it came so quickly that Gifford's moustache could scarcely cover the smile that was lurking in the corner of his lips. He knew that she must have been aware of his presence,—watching him through a chink in the *karakami* doubtless.

She came in, made her bows and took her seat as before. Then Gifford produced his sketches, and laid them one by one before Mr. Tanaka, explaining all the time. Of course his explanation to reach the old gentleman had to pass through Ayame's lips. In half-an hour she was listening to him with flushed cheeks and heaving breast, plying him with questions on her own account and so carried away by his recitals that from time to time she forgot her duties as interpreter, and had to be reminded by her uncle that he also wished to know what Mr. Gifford was saying.

The initial sketches were amateurish work dating away back from the middle of the seventies. The first things that excited attention were a few lurid episodes of the Russo-Turkish War of '77-78, in which Gifford had contrived to lay the foundation of his newspaper connection. Then came such subjects as 'Defence of Rorke's Drift,' 'Execution of Sophia Perovskaia and other Nihilists,' 'A Zouave charge in the Tunisian Desert,' 'McNeil's Zareba,' 'Burman Dacoits at Work,' followed by a whole crowd of

pieces, that demanded much explanation to make
their meaning clear, and much speaking

> *Of most disastrous chances,*
> *Of moving accidents by flood and field ;*
> *Of hair-breadth 'scapes i' the imminent deadly breach ;*
> *Of being taken by the insolent foe*
> *And sold to slavery.*

For as a matter of sober fact one of the pictures
he shewed had been limned while the gentle-minded
followers of Cetywayo were holding a palaver
whether they should butcher the artist out of hand
or keep him for further amusement and diversion.

In spite of himself, and apparently all unwillingly,
Gifford had to dilate on the personal factor in connection with his work. Yet at first he was modest
withal, and kept himself as far as he could in the back-
ground. But as he proceeded Ayame was not
content to let him remain there. She would insist
on knowing the part he had played in the scenes he
had depicted. So seemingly perforce he talked of
himself.

And it was a good deal more than little of this great
world he could speak. Nor did it all pertain to feats
of broil and battle. Court life at St. Petersburg,
artistic Bohemianism in the Quarter Latin, Faran-
doles in Provence, Stock-riding and Gold-mining
and Bêche de Mer fishing in Australia,—all these
and more he had limned from actual participation

in, and personal acquaintance with. It was not
merely a case of the Moor and Desdemona over
again. It was rather a Scoto-American Odysseus
with a point to make, working up to that point in a
way far too subtle to ever occur to the simple-
minded, puzzled-headed Othello. For Gifford both
could and did employ the easy and flowing and
winning words of the cunning subverter of Troy,
who worked his own sweet will upon Kalypso and
eke upon Circe herself,—that will going even beyond limning their unadorned charms, which was
Gifford's sole and single object in the present
instance.

It was almost dusk when he finished his recital.
Then dead silence felt on both his listeners. Ayame
and her uncle sat spell-bound alike as the shadows
thickened around them. When Gifford rose to go
he was again pressed to come next day.

"Had he more pictures?" asked Mr. Tanaka
as eagerly as etiquette would allow.

Gifford said he had.

"Then please to honour me and bring them that
I may honourably look at them!" translated Ayame.

As the painter replaced his portfolio among the
litter of his luggage in the bungalow, and lit the
lamp he muttered :—

"So much for a beginning. It's not a big opening perhaps, but I dare say it will serve."

X.

Next morning he was early astir and at work. During the forenoon a face gradually gave promise of coming into being on his easel. At noon he stopped for a rest. He again scrutinised the result of his labours and once more he had serious misgivings. However this time he kept violent hands off his work.

He lunched, and after lounging for an hour on the verandah perusing a reprint of Latimer's Sermons he happened to have among his queerly assorted traps, he leisurely picked out another assortment of sketches from his impedimenta. In a few minutes he again presented himself at the wicket-gate of the front entrance of the villa. As he was about to announce his presence by the usual *o tanomi moshimasu*, Santaro greeted him. The little fellow had already to a great extent recovered from the attentions of his Crabship. He dragged Gifford off through the gate in the hedge to the left, and over the lawn in front of the house to its far corner. The artist found himself on an archery-ground with a target in front of him—a diminutive disc it was, but the range was also Lilliputian—and a bow in his hand, thrust there by Santaro. As he was turning it over and over, Mr. Tanaka and Ayame appeared on the scene. Santaro seemed to get a mild scolding for his officiousness while the artist was the recipient of profuse apologies therefor. Then Gifford fixed an arrow on the string and fired. He aimed at the target, and succeeded in hitting a rooster on a neighbouring fence, much to that worthy fowl's astonishment and discomposure. This of course meant a general chorus of laughter, from all save the fowl, and then Tanaka san stepped forward and taking the bow showed Gifford how to handle it after the Japanese fashion.

Now this happens to be radically different from the English way, both in the release and also in the holding of the bow. Gifford saw at a glance that with the Japanese, archery is all pure arm-work. Now as luck would have it, that afternoon he had just read in Latimer;—" *My father was de-*

lighted to teach me to shoot with the bow. He taught me how to draw, how to lay my body to the bow, not to draw with strength of arm as other nations do, but with the strength of the body." So mindful of that, after one or two vain attempts to launch unerring shafts *more Japonico* he fell back upon the doughty old Bishop's homily on how to shoot, and laying the major portion of twelve stone weight upon the bow, he drew the arrow to the head and let loose. It sprang from the string, and literally sang though the air. It did not hit the mark by a good way, but it served to give some idea of the virtue contained in beef and beer. Gifford took another shot and another, and at last picking out the longest shaft he could find he planted it in the outer ring of the target. It tore through it and buried itself up to the feather in the bank behind.

"My Uncle says *that* as for skill in hitting, you perhaps want practice. As for strength, it is more than Tametomo or Benkei!"

Her eyes glistened as she said this.

"*So desu ka?* thought Gifford to himself. "It's the same all the world over. It's strength and might and power the darlings ever set their hearts upon."

But he did not say as much. He merely acknowledged the compliment by a smile and then handed the bow to Mr. Tanaka.

The old gentleman slipped his garments from his left shoulder, exposing his chest and his left ribs to the waist. Then he drew on the *yu-gake* and knotted it's strings about his wrist, chose out a shaft and fitting the notch on the string took his stand on the outspread mat. He raised the bow above his head, and then lowered it till it was on a level with his upper lip, drawing at it all the while. When the arrow lay level with his cheek, just as the bow reached it's stretch,

he loosed, and the shaft fell with a flop right in the bull.

Gifford clapped approval.

With a smile Tanaka san took up another arrow, and fitted it to the string and sent it to keep company beside the first, right in the innermost spot of the target. He followed this up with a third and a fourth, and then he called to Santaro to hand him another sheaf-ful.

Gifford had watched this narrowly all the time. It was not the old man's skill that drew his attention so much, for what Tanaka san had just done could be bettered in almost any *yumi-ya* (archery-booth) in the Capital. The artist's professional instinct was aroused; the fine clean old face with its firm lines, the spare yet sinewy ribs and the lean but muscular arm—Gifford noted the streak of shadow thrown upon it by the levelled shaft—and the general pose of the archer all challenged the cunning of his craft. So as his host made ready for a fifth shot Gifford turned quickly to Ayame.

"Ah," said he to her, "please ask Mr. Tanaka to stand for a minute."

He opened his portfolio, fixed a sheet of rough paper in position, and set to work with the charcoal.

"*Ha! Ha! So desu ka?*" said Tanaka san, with an approving smile as he took in the situation at a flash.

Gifford worked carefully but at the same time rapidly. He was afraid of tasking the old gentleman's patience and good-nature too far however, and asked Ayame to convey as much to him in the politest terms. He paused for a moment and Tanaka san looked at his handiwork. It evidently pleased him highly. Through Ayame he complimented the artist and then he proposed a resumption of the work after some refreshment.

Accordingly they adjourned to the *kyaku-ma* (guest-room) where Gifford again shewed more sketches. This time it was Russian Prison scenes, some of his Japanese work, and what he had not produced in his first visit, some sketches of the nude ;—a Venus dei Medici, a Venus after the bath, Chloe, Haidee, and the kindred subjects the cheesemonger's wife would insist on banishing from art saloons and public picture galleries. He keenly noted the effect of them on Ayame. The only emotion it seemed to arouse was curiosity. No silly blushing, no mawkish awkwardness ; as he went on pointing out beauties of contour, pose and proportion, he could see that she was following him closely and appreciating all that he said. She was especially attracted by his sketch of the Venus dei Medici.

"What a beautiful woman that is ! Surely you must love her very much," she said simply enough, yet with the slightest suspicion of a tremor in her tones that was unto Gifford's ear as the sweetest music.

He said he *did* love her very much, but that unfortunately such women no longer existed in the flesh. He was on the point of making an exception to this sweeping statement in favour of present company; but he pulled himself up sharp and stifled the words remorselessly. His instinct told him that any flattery of this description would be a false note, so he merely explained about the statue, its history, and its divine magnificence. He then did venture a little distance on the path he meant to take.

"Ah!" he said with a sigh, "if a poor painter of these modern times could light on a goddess-like woman such as this, what a glory for his art it would be! I, poor unworthy dauber as I am, would give years of my life for such a chance."

"But have you not seen women as beautiful as she?" queried Ayame hesitatingly.

"I think that in all my life-time I have met one only that could compare with this for a moment," he answered slowly and quietly, and in a tone that seemed to regret that she could not be a subject for his brush. Ayame looked at him inquiringly, but he quickly changed the theme of conversation.

After he had gone through his portfolio, he asked Mr. Tanaka if he now felt inclined to have his picture finished. Tanaka san spoke a few hurried words to Ayame, and then made a prostration to Gifford. The girl turned to him with a flushed face.

"My uncle," she began, "says *that*:—It is much inconvenience he gives you. Our house is a poor and narrow one, therefore he has much fear in telling what he tells. But would you please send for all your luggage and bring it here, and stay in our unworthy house till that time of the return of your friend? He says *that*."

Gifford's heart gave a throb of joy at the invitation. But he was careful not to seem over-eager to accept it. He bowed and said that they did him much honour, but that he feared his coming would give them trouble. Ayame protested that it would not do anything of the kind. Then he agreed and that evening he dined with Mr. Tanaka and that night slept on his best *futon* in the drawing-room.

XI.

Next forenoon he finished his study of the archer.
As he put the finishing touches to it, the old painter
watched him intently. At last Gifford looked at the
thing with a sigh; he could do no more with it.
He blew his fixitive over it, and handed it to his
host. The gift was accepted with a series of bows
and a shower of compliments.

That afternoon the old painter had to go down into
the village on business. It was evidently with the
Doctor he had to transact it, for Gifford saw him in
the ferry-boat crossing the reach that lay in front of
the medico's house on the spit between the two

arms into which the inner harbour divided. Shortly afterwards he found himself on the lawn, alone with Ayame.

In the morning after breakfast, he had noticed her casting longing eyes at the volumes O'Rafferty maliciously asserted he carried round with him as so many soporofics. For some of them were indeed heavy reading. But some of them were not, and these he had offered to Ayame. Among them was Butcher and Lang's Translation of the Odyssey, and what time she had not passed in company with Gifford that morning she had spent over its magic words. When she came forth on the lawn she brought this volume with her. She sat down on the grass near Gifford and laid the book beside her.

"Ah!" said the artist. "You like Odysseus do you not?"

"As for this book it is very wonderful, but in places I do not quite understand. But it must be very fine to travel like this man,—and you."

She added the last two words with the slightest tinge of hesitation.

"Do you think so?" he asked. "Would you like to travel?"

"Yes!" she said almost with a gasp. "What a life to be like yours and to see all that you have told. But then you are a man, and it is a man's life to do so."

This she said slowly and deliberately, as if weighing the matter fully. Then she went on ;—

"What do you think the end of life is? Power, —like our Taiko, or Yoritomo perhaps?"

Gifford was utterly taken aback at this break. From the earnestness of her tones it was pretty evident it was no mere haphazard question. It was staggering to be put through an examination on teleology in halting Eenglish by a Japanese girl of eighteen or nineteen who had never been away from her guardian's roof.

"What do you mean exactly?" he inquired after a slight pause.

"My teacher said *that* it was to be happy, and my uncle says *that* it is to be great. But as for you, how do you think?" she proceeded.

The painter was still in doubt as to whether he should answer seriously or treat the matter jestingly.

"I fear I talk nonsense," she said with a blush. "Pardon me if I ask a rude question. I do not well understand foreign manners, and perhaps I have made an impoliteness."

Gifford hastened to assure her that she had made nothing of the sort, but said that her question was difficult to answer in a few words.

"Do you know Evolution?" he asked tentatively.

"Evolution! Yes, I know," she replied, nodding understandingly.

" Well, Evolution I think must decide for us what the end or aim of life should be."

He paused and looked at her, curious to see if he was not speaking to her in riddles.

"Well," she queried, " what does it teach us?"

" It says the law of your being is, 'Develop, develop, develop! Develop all your faculties,—physical, intellectual and moral—fully and harmoniously.'"

He fancied to himself that he had gone beyond her depth with this and he looked to see how she would flounder.

She paused for a minute as if thinking and then repeated his words, slowly one by one, like a countryman telling over coins, or counting a bundle of *yen* notes with unaccustomed fingers.

"That is difficult!" she said at last, after a minute's thought while Gifford gazed at her with wonder, as she sat there with her chin on her palm and her elbow on her knee, and the workings of her brain almost visible in her occipital muscles. " 'Harmoniously' I don't quite understand."

The painter tried to explain, but his exposition was not sufficiently clear.

" Excuse me, but I give you much trouble. I will find a dictionary."

She rose and tripped off over the lawn to the

house. Gifford's gaze followed her with admiring astonishment.

"Here's a find!" he muttered to himself. "What would they say to this in a Boston drawing-room, the home of 'culchah,' I wonder?"

But after all, the thing was not by any means so extraordinary as it seemed. For Tanaka san had made a companion of his niece. And the old gentleman besides being an artist had a great fondness for science, and was like most Japanese, a voracious devourer of books. His favourite reading had been along biological lines, and among the many volumes he had assimilated were Japanese translations of Darwin and Haeckel. And many had been the evenings during which Ayame had read aloud from these tomes for his edification and amusement, delighting the old gentleman vastly the while by plying him with questions that put him on his mettle to answer, and that stimulated thought in no mean measure. But Gifford, of course, was ignorant of the fact. Wherefore he was overpowered and amazed.

Ayame returned with Hepburn's Dictionary almost immediately, and sitting down in her former position, hastily turned over the leaves.

"H. a." "har-mo-nious," she said to herself as she ran her finger over the page and brought it to a stop at the word.

She thought for a moment, apparently unconscious of everything around her.

"Ah! yes," she said, "I see. That is fine, but it
must be very difficult to carry out."

Then after another pause :

"But there is one thing you care for more than
others?" she asked at last. "For instance my uncle
despises money, but would die for his art."

"I understand that," said Gifford almost enthu-
siastically, "and I sympathize with him from the
bottom of my heart. My art is the thing I live for
above all others. And what do *you* consider the
aim of life to be?" he asked with unspeakable
curiosity.

"What do I think the aim of life to be?" she repeated almost sadly. "I am a woman, and in Japan
woman is weak. The Greater Learning for women
says *that*,—'Because it is a girl's end, when she
becomes a woman, to go to a new house, and be
obedient to her husband's father and mother, it is
still more her duty than a boy to listen to the
teaching of her honourable parent. It is the chief
duty of a girl living in the house of her parents to
practise piety toward her father and her mother, and
after marriage to love and reverence her husband's
father and mother with all her power, and to serve
them with every kind of piety.' And again it
says 'the life-long duty of a woman is obedience.'

It is not for the women of Japan, as for foreign women according to the saying of my teacher."

" That used to be the way with Western women, but they have changed all that ;—they are different now," said Gifford with keen amusement and a far-off remembrance of the epistle of one Paul to a Eurasian Bishop of the name of Timothy, and a vivid recollection of the fashion in which a little American missionary woman had ordered her husband to fetch and carry for her on the trip over from Shanghai.

"And again it says," went on Ayame, " *that,*— 'A woman should look on her husband as if he were a God, and never weary of thinking how that she may obey to her husband.' No! In Japan a woman is only a servant, and her duty is to only obey all her life."

Gifford smiled inwardly as he bethought him of the manner in which Kreon would have lifted the roof of a Japanese *shibai* (theatre) with applause should it have been given unto him to mouth his ἐμοῦ δὲ ζῶοντος οὐκ ἄρξει γυνή on the boards of the Shinto-miza or the Kabukiza in Tokyo.

"But is it not good for a woman to have a husband?" he asked, to draw her out still further.

" Good? Of course. For here in Japan no women are independent save the *geisha*, and my uncle says *that* they are now despised and that they

have changed much from the ancient time. A
woman can do nothing by herself. And this that
I have read in your book to-day is fine. It is the
saying of the hero Odysseus to the daughter of the
king."

She took up the Odyssey and opened it at the
place at once. Gifford noticed that she had put a
tiny paper marker between the leaves at the passage. She read out slowly as if at an elocution
lesson;—'*And may the gods grant thee all thy
heart's desire: a husband and a home, and a mind
at one with his may he give—a good gift, for there
is nothing mightier and nobler than when man and
wife are of one heart and mind in a house, a grief
to their foes, and to their friends great joy, but their
own hearts know it best.*'

She looked up with a flush on her face.

"Excuse me!" said the painter with a smile,
"lend me the book for a minute."

He took it and turned back a few leaves.

"And thus it may be with you," he said. And
in his turn he read out:—

"*Lo, already they are wooing thee, the noblest
youths of all the Phæacians, amongst that people
whence thou thyself dost draw thy lineage.*"

She flushed a brighter red than before, and then
the blood sank out of her face and sadness grew and
welled up in her eyes.

"The noblest youths of the land!" she said with
a tinge of bitterness that almost amounted to irony.
"No, indeed! It is only Ishida san, the old doctor,
who comes to ask me for his son!"

Gifford started in spite of himself. O'Rafferty's
words came back upon him like a flash, while the
grounds of the old quack's visit and of Tanaka san's
anger on the day before were now as clear to him
as if written in ten-inch capitals.

"His son? What is he like? Is he short and
dark, with a frock-coat and white waist-coat and
many rings and chains and———"

"Yes, it must be that man!"

A look came over the painter's face that meant
things might become awkward for Ishida san the
younger under certain circumstances.

"But," broke in Ayame quickly, evidently feeling
that they were on delicate ground and thinking
well to change it, "who was that very beautiful
woman you said that you had seen, and whom
you wished to draw? Pardon me, if I ask a rude
thing," she added almost confusedly.

"A rude thing! Certainly it is not a rude thing
to ask. But will you pardon me, if I say a rude
thing, when I say it is *you*."

A dead silence fell upon them both. Ayame's face
was again a study. She seemingly retired within
herself, thinking and trying to see her way clearly.

"You wish to draw me like that other statue," she said slowly at last. Gifford scarcely noticed the 'other;' the word caught his attention afterwards.

"Yes," he said. "I do!"

"Then do you think it would be good for your art?" was her next question.

"Good for my art! It would be a chance of which I have never had the like and never shall again."

She again paused for a moment.

"Well, I cannot say, but I will tell my uncle and ask him. I see him coming up the mountain."

When Tanaka san entered she followed him into the house. Gifford sat on pins and needles all the time. If his shot missed, the only thing that remained for him, he knew, was to take his leave as gracefully as he could.

In a quarter of an hour she reappeared.

"My uncle says that it is good, but that you must not call the picture by my name, and that he will be present."

Gifford's heart gave a great leap. His cast had won.

Next morning Gifford fixed his easel at the door of the *furoba*. As he was doing so, he happened to glance over in the direction of the lighthouse. He saw someone in front of his deserted bungalow, with his hands in front of his eyes, as if raking his own position with a binocular. He had the best grounds for knowing that his position *could* be raked from the other side, so he looked about for the wherewithal to erect defences. With a door and a curtain he succeeded in his object, and then he re-addressed himself to his preparations.

He was just about to begin when a crunching on the gravel of the path and a startled cry from Ayame made him turn round. There was an intruder; no less than the Europeanized dandy Gifford had seen being ministered to by the triad of Hebes in the *chaya* on the slope two days before. He came forward, bowing and smirking and smiling, but with a leer on his face. Gifford advanced to meet him, and met his bows with antiphonal bobs, backing him towards the fence all the time, out of sight of the door-of the bath-house. Then all of sudden he straightened himself, sprang upon him and seized him by the nape of the neck as he would a cat and lifted him over the fence. There happened to be an undergrowth of prickly shrubs on the very spot where he was dropped.

Then the artist coolly returned to his occupation. All that day and the next and the next he kept closely at work. Mr. Tanaka was in almost constant attendance.

On the sixth morning after his first visit to the

house Gifford awoke with a heavy heart. The whole household appeared to be depressed. As usual the painter worked hard throughout the day ; then in the evening he and Ayame strolled out upon the bluff.

They said but little in words, for in a measure words were unnecessary. They had reached that stage of friendship and intimacy where a tone, a look, a touch meant more than vocables could convey. They watched the sun's rim dip redly behind the shoulder of Fuji, and the whole landscape flush in an after-glow of crimson-violet, with nought around them but silence. The twilight was darkening into the dusk when they found themselves under an old gnarled pine, with the balmy evening wind voicing a gentle and soothing melody among his shivering needles overhead.

As they stood there on the brow of the cliff watching the light flashing out over the darkling deep, something like a great white bird of night rounded the base of the island crag and with outspread wings came flitting over the surface of the water. Then followed a series of shrill whistle-blasts, and with a creaking of blocks the pinions dropped from sight. A few hoarse calls and answers, a great splash as the anchor went down, and the *Komachi* rode once more at her moorings.

" Co-e-e ey !" rang out in long ear-splitting wail

the Australian call-note of the bush. Ayame san clasped Gifford's hand still more tightly and shivered. In spite of himself the artist felt as if a chill had fallen on him. Again the cry was given, followed by an Irish view halloo.

"Why the divil don't yez rispond?"

Thus adjured Gifford answered.

"Av course I knew you would be there or thereabouts. Now I'll tell yez. I'll give yez all tonight to say adieu. We start at three in the mornin'. Your boat goes at noon, but mine sails three hours before that."

"Yours?" asked Gifford in amazement.

"Yes, that's pwhat I said. Some man in Australia has been makin' free wid me dividends, an' I've tu find out the party an' interview him widout delay. I'll tell yez whin you're at leisure. Goodnight an' don't dishturb me ripose when yez come on board."

This was said in a tone that indicated no reply was either necessary or desired.

For a moment Gifford gazed gloomily upon the murky waters below. Ayame's fingers tightened still closer on his arm. He looked down to find her face raised to his with her two great eyes swimming with tears. He bent his head, and her lips met his.

XII.

The darkness was joining futile issue with the dawn as Gifford scrambled on board. Without waking O'Rafferty from his stertorous slumbers below, he got Koto the *sendo* to understand that he wished to have his impedimenta brought down from the villa. Koto got over the side into the dingy and rowed off into the fog that was resting on the water like a great pall of white. In ten minutes, all the artist's luggage was on the deck. Koto dropped the easel as he put it down; its clatter roused O'Rafferty from his dreams. He jumped up at once, and thrust his night-cap from the companion-way.

"Hallo!" he said. "An so ye're just off the tiles are yez? Well, it's a purty an' innocint young maan yez luk! Yo ho! All aboard, up anchor, hoist sail, an off we are from the scene av yer manifold iniquities!"

Gifford merely muttered some inconsequent reply. He sat down and looked moodily and absent-mindedly into the bank of mist that now swathed the cliff from its middle upwards.

"Av course ye've accomplished your own artistic purpose, haven't yez?" queried O'Rafferty as he lit his pipe and took hold of the tiller.

"Ye've painted her purty picture ;—av course wid an abundant paucity av raiment, haven't yez?" he went on, giving but scant attention to Gifford's absorption.

"No!" was all he got for answer ; and shortly and curtly it was uttered.

"Phwhat!" he said slowly, looking over at his friend keenly but quizzically. "I thought 'twas a hundred *yen* a month ye were tu give her tu pose fur yez. Well now by my calculation it's just over six days av her society ye've had. So by the rule av aliquot parts it's just a thrifle av twinty *yen* ye'll have paid her,—that is widout counting in the *hana*."

"Confound your thick pate! Can't you take a

hint, man, and hold your tongue?" said Gifford
angrily and impatiently, and evidently looking for
something to throw.

"Whee-ew" whistled O'Rafferty. "It's serious.
An' it's actually baadly shtruck in a tinder part he is!"

Then turning away, and removing the pipe from
his mouth he sung softly and feelingly over the stern,
yet audibly enough for his friend to hear :—

> "*Bonnie Charlie's noo awa*
> *Sailin' ower the ragin' main;*
> *O! my heart 'ull break in twa*
> *Should he no come back again.*"

Then turning round again, and looking down into
his lap, and as if speaking to himself, he proceeded :—

"Thy neck is as a tower av ivory, thine oiyes
loike the fish-pools in Heshbon by the gate av
Beth-rabbim ; thine head upon thee is loike Kyarmel,
and the hair av thine head loike purple, an' it's me
pore frind Gifford that's tangled in its purty meshes
past all human power av redimption!"

Just then they passed out through the harbour-
entrance. The mist lifted as the sun began to
mount from his bath in the ocean. Gifford looked
anxiously up at the cliff. But he saw nothing, for
the villa was too far back to be within the range of
his vision. But on the verandah of one of the neighbouring houses, which commanded a prospect of the

Komachi's course for some hundred yards after she had stood out past the lighthouse, Ayame stood following the yacht with tear-stained staining eyes. And as she vanished round the headland and even the ripples in her wake subsided into the monotonous levels of the sleeping sea, she pressed her hands upon her breast and wailed with great sobs ;—

" *Kite kudasaranakereba shinde shimaimasu yo!*"
(If you don't come back I shall die, I shall die!)

The Laird o' Cockpen he is proud an' he's
*   great ;*
His mind is ta'en up wi' the things o' the
*   state ;*
He wanted a wife his braw house to keep ;
But favour wi' wooin' was fashious to seek.

PART II.

I.

As the villas on the bluff vanished from their ken the painter's head sank forward on his chest. O'Rafferty had the grace to leave him alone till he came to himself. It was not till the *Komachi* was standing across Uraga Bay that Gifford roused himself from his abstraction.

"Here!" said O'Rafferty, who had been watching him with close side-glances all the time, "I've brought you your mail. Lay hould! An' it's not even thanks I ask fur me pains."

He threw over a sizeable packet towards the artist—mostly of newspapers and magazines. Gifford opened and went through his letters mechanically and with but little show of interest, and then he spread out one of his newspapers. He ran his eye down its columns and in one place shrugged his shoulders contemptuously. All at once he threw down the sheet and turned to his friend.

"Look here, old man!" he broke out. "I'm a regular brute!"

"Well, as it's yersilf fur whom I've unbounded respect that sez it, it's not mesilf that 'ull conthradict yez," said O'Rafferty cheerily. "An' besoides I've known it all along. But why are yez more conscious av the fact now than at other more saysonable toimes?"

"Because I fancy from what you said last night you're in something of a fix. What did you mean by saying that some one had been tampering with your dividends?"

"Just that as far as I can make out 'from information resaved' (here he mimicked the Irish colonial bobby on the witness-stand) that at the prisint moment all me possessions are summed up in a few hundred dollars in a Yokohama Bank, me thraps in the Club Hotel, the clothes I hev on me back and the *Komachi*. An' it's hersilf that I'm afraid I must part wid."

The final sentence of this deliverance was uttered with something that sounded like a tremor. Gifford at once saw that the case was really serious.

"Part with the *Komachi*! Nonsense, man!" he

said. "What has happened to make such a thing ever enter your harum-scarum head?"

"Happened! Only that every penny I had in the Broken Hill Moine has gone!"

"Gone? Stolen? Embezzled? How?"

"Swallowed, as far as I can make out."

"Swallowed! What do you mean, man? Don't talk in riddles."

"Swallowed up, I sez!"

"But how?"

"Swallowed up by a shark wid a big ugly mug, and cruel lookin' fins."

"Explain, man!"

"Well, you know me mate Johnson? He put me in the Moine and made me fortune. Well, whin I came away I gave him a Power av Attorney to sell out whin he thought fit, fur thim shares, yez must understand, are oncertain as the climate av Melbourne where the thermometer runs up from nothing to a hundred and tin, and folks pass from singlets to greatcoats widin wan short half-hour. Div yez moind me now?"

Gifford nodded comprehension.

"Well, thin, two months ago or more he sould out. 'Twas a mather av sivin an twinty thousand pounds he got, cash down in thousand pound notes,—sivin an' twinty av thim all tould and crisp."

"Well, what next?" asked Gifford, as O'Rafferty again came to a pause.

"Well, now it was a thafe av a Japanese *yakusha* that was to blame."

"A how much?" asked the painter with puzzled astonishment.

"A *yakusha*; that's what I said. And *yakusha* is Japanese fur an actor-maan, although it was wumman's parts he tould me he usually tuk."

"In the name of the Sphinx, how did a Japanese what-d'ye-call-'im ever come to be mixed up in the business?"

"It's a long story, but I can give yez the heads av the chapters. 'Twas this way:—Johnson an' mesilf whin we shtruck it rich, came up to Japan."

"Well?"

"Thin we bought a boat,—a yacht I mean. But she wasn't a patch on the *Komachi*. The *Komachi* is————"

"Oh! bother the *Komachi*; come to the point, man!"

"Well, we cruised about mostways, for she— the other boat that was—waz a biggish craft, sea-going in fact. Johnson sailed her home tu Australia. Well, wan night we were anchored in the bay, not far off Kanagawa when a fellow cloimbed on board out av the bowels av the deep. We were still engaged in interviewin' him whin the wather-

police came alongside and asked if we had seen any
wan loike him. He wint down on his marrow-
bones and asked us to lie to save him, and we did.
That was the actor chap I spoke av. He had got
mixed up wid some *geisha* gurls in Kioto, an'
had engaged in an animated discussion wid wan
about politics in the course av which he had
made use av a Japanese small sword as an
argument, an' the gurl died. But accordin' tu
himsilf he wasn't tu blame, tho' the authorities
moight have thought different. You see in the
mather av the wummen now, ever since the widdey
bruk me—"

"Heart! I know. All right. But about this what
d'ye-call-him,—this actor man?"

"Oh, the actor maan! Well he begged tu be
tuk wid us tu Australia whin I tould him we were goin'
there. He said he'd do anything fur us an' would
want no wages at all. He'd go as *boy*-san or *sendo*
or anything we loiked. Well, Johnson though a
dimmycrat, thought a body-servant would be a
tony thing, more beloike if that silf-same body-servant were an outlandish haythen Japanese. Besoides
he thought it would be a good advertisement fur
him, fur Johnson is business all over. An' so he
made a sort av confidential clerk av him whin he
had learned English, which he tuk up like a rooster
feedin' on corn. Besoides that, Johnson had him

wait at table whin his lady frinds came tu dinner av an evenin', fur Johnson's a 'cute man an' knows what's in appearances. So though he knows no more Japanese than yersilf, which is less than nought, he entertains his company wid dissolvin' views av his erudition, an' turns to the Japanese wid gibberish that's worse than Hottentot clicks. But the *yakusha* enters into the joke and by way av flatterin' Johnson an' makin' him look loike a pundit, he grins and bobs and bows and says '*Sayo, sayo!* *Sayo de gozaimasu!*' An' all the wimmen folks, they just all get shtruck on Johnson in consequence av his linguistic ability."

"A smart fellow, this actor would seem to be," muttered Gifford

"Smart!" went on O'Rafferty catching his words. "Smart isn't the word for it. What do you think av that fur a maan that's been studdyin' English fur less than two years? There's not a mistake in it, and the penmanship is wonderful. I got that nine months or so ago."

He extracted a letter from a corpulent pocket-book and handed it across to the painter. Gifford glanced over it hurriedly; as O'Rafferty said the English was perfect and the penmanship striking, with a bold and strong individuality of its own. It was an epistle thanking the Irishman for the service rendered to the writer, and protesting that he would never forget his kindness, and so on, with a lot of appropriate frilling.

"H'm!" said Gifford, handing it back. "What next?"

"Well!" said O'Rafferty, tearing up the sheet preparatory to throwing it overboard. "As I'll have to go loight-armed from now, it's well to dispose av all shuparfluous thraps. So there———"

"Stop!" almost shouted Gifford, jumping up. "What are you doing?"

"Why, clearin' away the rubbish, to be sure!" said O'Rafferty in wonderment at the artist's sudden energy.

"Well then, don't begin with that. Keep it, and keep it carefully. It may come in handy yet. Now, go on!" he said, sinking back against the bulwark again.

"Anything tu plaze yez!" said O'Rafferty somewhat testily as he replaced the fragments in a fold of the pocket-book. "Well, I said it was this Japanee that lost me money. And it was this way. 'Twas a rich miner that bought me clame and he paid in Bank-notes. It was too late tu put the money in the bank an' Johnson gave it to Takahashi to take it home an' diposit it in the safe in his house. His house is beyant the harbour an' Takahashi wint in the ferry-boat. Now there was a collision, an the boat got the worst av it, bein' shtruck in the pit av her stomach, and wint tu the bottom av the say.

An' it bein' afther dark there's no sayin' pwhat happened. But anyhow all the passengers were
picked up savin' the Japanese, and nought was ever
more seen av his person 'ceptin' his hat."

" Drowned? put in Gifford.

" More beloike drowned an' thin devoured by
the sharks. They're powerful big wans, are Sydney
sharks, an' not at all particular to their feed
either, bein' ready fur anything from ould tin-inch
nails tu Christians, let alone a haythen Japanese."

" And your money was in his pocket?"

" Av course! 'Twas an expinsive dinner the baste
tuk!"

" Humph! I should say so. One at Delmonico's
would not be a patch on that. But, (here Gifford
spoke very slowly and distinctly and looked O'Rafferty right between the eyes) *are you quite sure
that the Japanese was either drowned or devoured?*"

" They sez it was so, and they should know.
They've been dredgin' for him, and besoides the
detectives have got the mather in hand."

" What have *they* done, do you know?"

" Telegraphed a description av the missin' maan
to all parts at which the next China boat stopped
on her way to Hong-kong, an' sent a maan along
that route."

" Humph! Much good that will do!"

" They think if he has by any possibility escaped,

he'll make fur Japan, 'cause there's no extradition wid the counthry."

"Of course they do! But do you think so? What about that 'political argument' with the *geisha*? Do they know about that?"

"Faith thin', they don't! An' if he's alive it's not tu Japan he'll come. Besoides he knows I'm here."

"Well and good! Now what are you going to do?"

"Why, off and up by the next boat to Australia. The *Werder* goes to-day to Hong-Kong and I'll get the Australian boat there. I'll have tu wait a fortnight there, hangin' me heels an' bitin' me thumbs an' gettin' roasted."

"How long from there to Sydney?"

"A mather av foive an' twinty days, what wid callin' at ports."

"Altogether seven weeks. O'Rafferty, my man, you're a good tactician, but your strategy is somewhat behind-hand."

"Well, isn't it mesilf that has always allowed that it's that silfsame strathegy ye're good fur? An' it's a pore maan that is good fur nothing. What have *you* got to say about the mather?"

"To begin with, that you are not to go on the *Werder* to Hong-Kong!"

"Well?" said O'Rafferty very drily, and stiffening his back ominously. "An' nixt?"

"And next, that you are to come with me to Vancouver," added Gifford quietly.

"*Pwhat?*" burst out the Irishman excitedly. "Do yez call that shtuff shtrategy? If that's a sample av it——"

"Stop now!" interrupted Gifford. "From here to Vancouver is about a fortnight, from there to 'Frisco less than three days, and from there to Australia, if your wrong-headness *will* take you there, about twenty-five days,—altogether shorter than by the other route."

"Yes, by the wink av an eyelash maybe. An' what other advantage is there in't?"

"You'll have the pleasure of my company for part of the way."

"Well, that's something! Anything else?" queried O'Rafferty ironically.

"Yes, a mere trifle though, perhaps!" replied Gifford taking up the newspaper he had thrown contemptuously aside, and at which he had been darting side-glances during the dialogue.

"Well, out wid it!"

"It is only I think you'll find your man not a corpse in a shark's belly, but alive in San Francisco, posing as a Japanese Daimiyo and keeping up state and style on the fag-end of the seven and twenty thousand-pound bank-notes you lament so sorely."

O'Rafferty jumped up and almost let go the
Komachi's tiller.

"Keep cool," said Gifford, "and listen to this."

He read out as follows.

"On the *Zealandia* which arrived from Honolulu
on the 24th, was Prince Matsudaira of Japan. He
is the owner of extensive estates round Fusi-yama,
and is we believe the Lord of that district. He is
a young man of prepossessing appearance, dignified
and courteous manners, with the hall mark of high
breeding and ancient lineage stamped on him in a
manner there is no mistaking . . . . . . "

The article, which in the main was an average specimen of the great and glowing and the same time re-
markably free-and-easy style of our own American in-
terviewing reporter, then went on with abundance of
detail to tell of His Highness' rooms in the Palace
Hotel, his sayings and doings there, and the intent and
purpose of his visit to 'these shores'. This was briefly
to 'study our civilisation and to introduce it among
his retainers!' All this and much more of a like cast
filled up a big proportion of a column in small pica,
adorned of course with catch words and head-lines
liberally distributed down the body of this wonderful
piece of copy.

"Now, then," said Gifford grimly "is not the
immortal interviewer a great and a grand institution! The Daimiyo of Fuji-yama! Only think

of it! Our actor friend is a humourist of a high order."

"Let me see it!" said O'Rafferty clutching the sheet eagerly. He ran his eye rapidly over it, and then he again went over it slowly and line by line.

"The Divil!" he gasped at last. "An' here while we're anxiously and wid much rigrit prospectin' fur the fragmints av his corpse in the bowels av a shark, here he is supportin' the style av the loftiest Lordship in Japan upon the money I've earned wid the the swate av me brow! Ow! let me just get at the spalpeen, an' it's mesilf that'ull Daimiyo av Fusiyama him!"

"Now just hold on a bit, you mad Irishman!" said Gifford waving him down into his seat with a restraining motion of his hand. "It is not by any means a sure thing that your actor and the Daimiyo of Fujiyama are one and the same. But there is no harm in looking into the matter and you can do that by coming with me. Of course you have every thing settled to start?

"All 'cept havin' got me money fur the *Komachi*," answered O'Rafferty with a shake in his voice.

"*What!*" responded Gifford more than severely. "Sold the *Komachi!* You haven't done that have you, surely?"

"Faith thin, an' I have," replied the other, actually with the tears welling up his eyes. "An' the baste

I've sould her tu is a lubber that'ull as loikely as not treat her despoitefully an' mishandle her, an' ruin her ripytashun, an' lose every race he sails wid her. But,—" here he really and truly blubbered outright,—"what else was I tu do? Tell me that if you plaze! Fur I'm as good as stone-broke!"

"Thanks for the compliment you've paid me, old man!" interrupted the artist drily. "If 5,000 dollars are any good to you, draw on me, and don't treat the *Komachi* as a hard-up Japanese trader would his daughter. Don't sell her into a life of immoral courses. And be blanked to you if you say a word of thanks. I'll punch your ugly head for you if you try to."

"It'll take a better maan than your own mother's son to do *that*," said O'Rafferty hastily, dashing the back of his hand across his eyes. Then stretching and seizing over Gifford's right he squeezed it passing forcibly.

"O'Rafferty," quietly said Gifford, holding up his hand and looking tenderly at his digits as he slowly spread them out. "You *are* a strong man, although you go on like a baby."

That afternoon the *Parthia* steamed out past the Susaki light-house with Gifford and O'Rafferty in the first cabin.

II.

In the middle of the summer of '90, there was an
unusual stir in political circles throughout the Empire of Japan.   Tailor Ito and his assistants, after a
visit to Berlin to make personal note of the latest
fashions in Clothes Constitutional had come back and
set to work to contrive and cut out and stitch together a brand new suit for the Land of the Rising
Sun.   It was the first outfit of the kind ever turned
out in Asia, and consequently when it was first
solemnly exposed to view in the early months of
'89, there had been great doings.   The occasion
had been marked by high-jinks of all sorts, from
the murder of a minister down to the emptying of
saké vats, and the shouting of '*Banzai!*' till throats

were baked. So when it came to actually trying on the Jacob's-coat-like robes there was excitement.

There were three hundred members to be chosen to make a Lower Chamber, and 453,895 electors to choose them. That is to say each member had on an average to profess himself the humble servant of some 1,500 of his fellow-countrymen. Now all this and much more Ishida Shozo carefully took into account when he began to engineer matters electoral in behalf of his offspring. He picked out a constituency that was neither very rich nor very numerous. It contained little more than one-third the normal number of electors, less than 600 all told.

Mr. Ishida spent some time in getting to know all about the greater portion of these worthy gentlemen. Some of them, in fact a good many of them, he found held the same politics as himself. These politics might be compendiously described as 'agin the govermint.' As regards these individuals it only needed a little soft-soaping to bring them to the ballot-box on polling-day in their own *jinrikisha*. Then there was an opposition camp, which was moderately strong. The old gentlemen did not trouble himself much with this contingent. He rested content with directing the attention of his *sōshi* to its most active and objectionable members.

These *sōshi* form a great institution in Japan.

They are recruited mostly from the ranks of an unemployed too lazy to work. Their special *metier* would seem to lie in working out the salvation of the country politically and otherwise, on an original plan of their own,—originality being the cardinal one in Young Japan's category of the virtues. The chief point in their programme consists in a gallant and fearless neglect of appearances, personal and conventional. They walk abroad, in unkempt and and towsy garb, with ugly murderous-looking bludgeons. They turn up at meetings hostile to their party and break them up with these self-same lethal weapons, or with chairs or *geta*, or with anything else that may come handy. They way-lay opposition politicians and hammer them till the life all but

leaves them—that is, when it is a case of half-a-dozen to one—and they take forcible possession of, and gut the offices of such newspapers as cannot afford to indulge in the luxury of a fighting-editor in the person of a wrestler. They sometimes vary these items in a comparatively inoffensive play-bill by invading houses with nobody in them but helpless women, and compelling them to furnish forth feasts, by assaulting legislators even within the precincts of the Diet,—and occasionally by going to jail, although not by any means sufficiently often to please a peace-loving and unappreciative public. Ishida san had some half dozen of these worthies retained at a moderate fee, for the old quack was not the man to waste good money recklessly.

But of the six hundred voters in the constituency there was a big sprinkling with politics of no colour at all. It was among these that Ishida san was especially busy. Being a wise man he made feasts and these fools ate them, in strict keeping with the old adage, for everything in Japan has to be taken upside-down,—proverbs included. When he rode out in state on electioneering business bent he didn't kiss the baby, because kissing and such on-goings are very bad form in Japan. But he did what was better;—he brought him sweet-meats and play-things, and declared on his knees to every in-dividual father among these undecided and un-

enlightened wielders of the brand-new franchise
that his own particular scalp-locked *botchan* was
the finest and best behaved child in the whole
Prefecture.

These tactics carried the old intriguer a considerable way, but not quite far enough. There were
others whose convictions needed something more
substantial than *go-chiso* (feasts) and commendation
of the baby to give them a distinctive complex-
ion. The old doctor had the necessary medicine
ready for this class also. Its Japanese name is
hanagusuri (nose-medicine), which means a bribe
in English. Not so long ago it was much used in
Oxford City and eke in Bridgewater Town, and in
America it is scarcely second in potency to St.
Jacob's Oil. This Mr. Ishida applied with judgment and deftness. And also with success; for
Ishida Taro came in at the head of the poll with
a thumping majority of 67 over the second man.

Having thus secured a seat in the prospective
Legislative Factory of the Empire, Ishida Taro thought
well to prosecute his suit with redoubled rigour.
Accordingly Ishida Shozo was busy. For in Dai
Nippon John does not speak for himself. He
must not, durst not, speak for himself. To do so
would be contrary to etiquette and convention; and
etiquette and convention are supreme in the land.
In this country the wooing of Miles Standish would

be *comme il faut;* only no Japanese swain would be so far lacking in common-sense as to send one younger and better looking than himself as ambassador plenipotentiary. He invariably depends upon the kind services of some one old and discreet,—some one with whom love and passion are but pleasing memories of a musty past. As likely as not it is an old professional matchmaker that he sends to maker soundings and to pop the question in his behalf. Not to the party most interested from our point of view, though. It is the father and mother, or the guardians of the damsel that are appealed to. Then if they think well of it, they signify their pleasure to the *Ojosama* (young lady) who has no resource but obedience.

Now inasmuch as Ishida Shozo had arranged many delicate affairs of this sort, in the course of a long and active and beneficent life, he charged himself with the suit of his son, Ishida Taro. He had got so far as broaching the subject on the very day of Gifford's second visit to the villa on the bluff. Although no direct reply was then vouchsafed him, he could see that Mr. Tanaka did not regard his proposal with much favour. But he was not unprepared for that, having foreseen as much from the very day the idea first entered his head. Accordingly he was ready with strategy to compass his purpose.

He returned for a definite reply some days after

Gifford had gone, and as he expected, received
' No ' for answer. Of course the refusal was toned
down and turned with the most punctilious but, at
the same time, cold politeness.

" Very much honour to our humble house,—overcome with awe at the proposal, etc. etc, etc., *but* the
unworthy niece did not wish to take a husband for a
long time yet."

When Mr. Tanaka had finished and ' done ' the
conventional phrases appropriate to the occasion,
his lips were compressed in a style eloquent of
finality,—from his ' unworthy side ' at least. But
Ishida Shozo, while thanking him for his answer,
and apologising for his presumption with his lips,
looked protest and war and menace with his shifty
fox-like smile. He bowed very low till his head
touched the floor, his hands outspread in deprecation on the mats in front of him, and then he arose
and hied him from the house.

Now Ishida Shozo was at once a man of many
wiles and of multifarious business. Besides being
a doctor, a land owner, a fishmonger, a money-
lender and a politician he was not above turning
an honest penny in any other way that offered.
He was a shining light in more than one of those
joint-stock undertakings that are for ever making
calls and never paying dividends ;—for all the world
just like a Queensland 'wild-cat' gold-mine. Then

besides he had a sleeping interest,—the 'sleeping' was done with both eyes wide open— in a big pawn-broking establishment in the metropolis. And besides all this, he was a bookseller and picture dealer although his name did not appear over the shop, and it was not generally known that he had anything whatsoever to do with the concern. But all the same, Hirata who ostensibly owned the establishment, was nothing but Ishida Shozo's *bantō* (managing-clerk).

Now it was to this Hirata that Tanaka san always sold his pictures. He had contracted with him to dispose of his productions to him and to no one else. There was a running account between them, which was supposed to be balanced and settled every June and December. When the usual half-yearly statement came in in June 1890, it appeared that Tanaka san was some four hundred *yen* to the bad. He had had to respond to a call from an old friend of his who was lying sick even unto death. The friend in question did die without leaving any assets to re-imburse Mr. Tanaka.

Now with this semi-annual statement of affairs had come a pretty plain request for an immediate settlement. This was altogether a new departure; besides the curtness of the note, regarded from a Japanese point of view went very close to amounting to an insult, and the artist's old *samurai* blood began to boil in his veins like water in a pot when the leaping tongues of fire are licking its belly. Thirty years ago he would have simply drawn his blade and sliced the fellow open from shoulder downwards. But things were ordered differently in the this twenty-third year of Meiji, with its New Codes, its brand-new Parliament, and its tendency to set the Golden Calf on high, at the expense of birth and worth alike. So he merely tore up the missive with a curl of contempt on his clean-cut lips, and sat down to write to declare the compact at an end.

But, as if some one had struck on his fifth-rib with the guard of a dirk, it came into his mind that he had not the wherewithal to comply with the demand for a settlement. Before the revolution *hara-kiri* would have easily settled all; but the days for that, as for many other excellent things of the past, were gone ; and besides there were Ayame and Santaro. The old man laid down the *fude* (brush) he was just preparing to dip in the *suzuri* (ink-stand), and gave himself up to reflection.

It was plainly a bitter moment. Evidently his thoughts were troubled as he sat there, with the bright July sunlight flushing the land with its glory and the cicalas in the shrubberies making the silence ring and quiver with the vibration of their mocking mirth.

At last he roused himself, opened his roll of letter paper, took up his brush and began to write. In a few minutes he had covered a four feet long strip of paper with six-inch vertical columns of the curves and hooks of a cursive script that was a wonder to be seen. He spread it out, and ran his eye over it hurriedly, and then taking up a scissors snipped it of from the roll, folded it up, thrust it into a long narrow straw-paper envelope, with the opening at one end, closed it and addressed it.

According to the general rule of topsy-turvey, the superscription began where the address on a European letter winds up. It ran as follows :—

Kanagawa-ken,
Miura-Gori,
Misaki-mura,
Sannaizaka 2257,
Ishida Shozo Mr.

The gist of this more than ell-long note was simply a request for Mr. Ishida to call on the writer, who wished to transact some business with him ; the balance of the superficies being occupied with the ordinary conventional formulæ so imperatively demanded by good Japanese epistolary style. For Tanaka san was a gentleman to the tip of his long left-hand little finger nail, and would never have dreamt of lapsing into the rude abrupt-

ness of young Japan, and the generation to which
he belonged was one not invaded by modern com-
mercial notions as to the value of time. Santaro
was summoned, and with many obeisances received
instructions to carry the missive down to the house
on the spit. With another low bow and a *kashikomarimashita*, (All right, honourable Sir!) the *botchan*
sped on his errand, and half an hour thereafter
Ishida Shozo presented himself at the *genka*.

He entered and seated himself on a cushion on
the mats and after the usual prostrations and suck-
ing in of breath he sat up and Tanaka san came to
the point.

"I am ashamed of giving you such trouble," he
began, "but as for those unworthy swords you
were pleased to admire some time ago, and which
I would not part with then, how is it now? I think
you said that an honourable friend of yours was
anxious to buy them."

Ishida Shozo could scarcely repress a smile of
delight as he put his head on one side, sucked in
his breath, and gave himself the air of one trying
to recall a circumstance that had escaped his recollection.

"Ha!" he says. "My poor and unworthy
memory was at fault. Perhaps it is those *Masa-
munes* and *Sukesadas* your Honour refers to?"

Tanaka san replied that it was.

"Well now," answered Mr. Ishida, "that is really unfortunate, because I am not sure if the gentleman I mentioned wishes to buy them any longer. But I will write and ask. And by the way, as for old embroideries and raiment, of which you have such a fine collection, I think my friend would be glad to buy."

Tanaka san looked at him closely. Ishida dropped his eyes, lit his pipe at the fire-box, took two long inhalations and then opening his lips allowed the fleecy smoke to pour out like a cloud of steam from the orifice of Oshima. He then rapped the *Kiseru* (pipe) on the edge of the brazier, partly to remove the ashes and partly to escape the other's searching glance.

"As for those swords now, there were twelve blades altogether I think. How much would your honour expect for them?" he asked at last.

"I beg to remark that I am not a merchant," said Tanaka san with cold pride. "How much will your friend give?"

Ishida Shozo darted a quick, ugly, shifty look from under his eye-brows at this. But he answered with humble politeness.

"Excuse me, if I have offended your honourable side. I do not know exactly until I write and ask, but I should say about 200 *mai*, because it is only the mountings that are valuable now. But I do not know for certain. I will ask."

Tanaka san thanked him for his trouble, and he soon rose and took his leave. The wrinkles of his old wizened face wreathed themselves into a simian grin as he closed the wicket behind him.

"Yes?" he muttered to himself. "I think I know the medicine that will cure this proud old Samurai pride of yours!"

And he hobbled off down the hill in the highest of high spirits.

In three days he sent up to say that on the following morning his friend in Tokyo would send an agent down to Tanaka san to negotiate for his swords and the fine garments he (Tanaka san) had spoken of. Now inasmuch as it was Ishida Shozo only who had mentioned the matter of the garments, the old artist thought that the old doctor's memory must really be weakening and getting confused.

Next day the 'agent' appeared. After a great deal of diplomacy he made an offer of 150 *yen* for the swords, which he ultimately raised to 170. He then referred to the clothes of which Mr. Ishida had spoken.

Now these were family heirlooms and it was with a heavy heart that Tanaka san asked Ayame to open the boxes in which they were stored. Not the smallest part of the ordeal this was to the old painter, was the tearful tone of Ayame's reply to his order. For the heirlooms were such as are dearest to the hearts of women. Some of them had been worn at festivals and weddings and funerals by maidens and matrons whose bones were already dust when Iyeyasu laced his helmet after Sekigahara, for Tanaka san had a family tree that went back to the time of the latter Hōjōs at Oda-wara. And now they were to go. It was a wrench. And so severe a wrench was it that at the very pinch the artist abruptly said he had changed his mind and meant to keep them.

Then with many bows and *osore-irimashita*'s the 'agent' humbly begged to be allowed to make a suggestion. 'Let them go as *shichi-motsu* to the *shichi-ya* (pledges to the pawn brokers.) For them he would advance 200 *yen;* at the end of six months your honourable side will easily redeem them.'

Ayame eagerly said that 'this would be good,' and on that understanding they were allowed to go. But Ayame's throat choked with sobs as the coolies carried them off through the gates, and down the slope and placed them on board Ishida Shozo's fish-carrying steamer to be deposited in the great Tokyo Mont de Piété, with its vaults, its coffers, and its pigeon-holes filled with the ruin and misery of countless families, all neatly arranged and ticketed with labels that knew no compassion.

The 'agent' could have told Ayame san that if her uncle failed to redeem them on the appointed day, the heirlooms of her house would as likely as not furnish forth the trappings of the scarlet women who sit in patience behind the bars of the cages in the Flower Quarters of the Capital.

But he didn't; for he even had saving grace,— had that 'agent' of Ishida Shozo's 'friend.'

III.

Things now began to go ill with Tanaka san.
When he settled the running account with Hirata
the picture-dealer, and broke off further transactions
with him, he found himself with a plentiful lack of
money. It was difficult for him to find a market
for his work. He made several journeys to Tokyo
to make arrangements elsewhere, but a month sped
without his being able to compass his end. So he

resolved to remove to the capital where he could press the matter more effectually.

He could not afford to live in any of the fashionable quarters on the ridges, so he went to Asakusa and there rented a house not far from the theatres. It was small and humble, for house-rent in Tokyo with its congested population is a different thing from what it is in a sea-coast village, and Tanaka san could not afford more than 4 *yen* per month for the loan of a roof. But though cribbed and confined it was ample for the wherewithal he now had left for its furnishing.

One single *ni-guruma* (hand-cart) was found sufficient to convey the meagre *dogu* (household) goods from the canal landing whither they had

been brought by boat, to his new and narrow
lodging. As the four *ninsoku* (coolies) piled
them on the vehicle and started off with their
strange antiphonal grunts of '*Hai! huida! ho!
ho! hai! huida! wo! ho! huida!*' of which no
mortal word-monger knoweth the etymology,
Ayame shivered in spite of herself and drew her
light shawl closer round her shoulders. And that
although the morning sun was shining strong. For
the scene he seemed literally to devour was not a
kindly one. How different from the Misaki pines
and the groves amid whose boughs and leaves his
beams played hide-and-seek as morning grew to noon
and noon waned to gloaming, and amidst which
the summer winds rustled and sighed and whispered,
pregnant with the refreshing of the ozone from the
darkling wine-faced deep. Here even the trees
and shrubbery seemed parched and athirst, dis-
reputable and unlovely in their stained and dust-
flecked foliage, with the long array of greasy,
weather-worn *kuruma*, and Lilliputian cook-stalls
redolent of cuttle-fish oil and poverty beneath them.
Then behind her was the muddy canal with its
unsightly slimy ooze, its fishy smells, and the
landing covered with ugly blocks of gritty friable
building-stone. It was a dismal prospect. Ayame
began to feel that in Tokyo things went hardly
with the poor.

And as time went on and the days lengthened
into weeks she felt it more and more. Her uncle
had been constrained to join himself unto a big
gofukuya, (drapery establishment) as a drawer of
designs for their fabrics. His work was incessant
and his remuneration 75 *sen* per day. On this it
was a struggle for the girl to make ends meet, while
all idea of rescuing the heirlooms of the house from
the pawn-broker's coffers faded rapidly indeed.
She never thought of them without a choking in
her throat, and in spite of herself the thought of
them often lay heavy upon her. For in her lone-
liness when Santaro was at school, and her uncle
at his work, time hung wearily upon her hands,
and her mind would run on themes that were not
cheering. Something heavier even than their
present evil case pressed ever upon her mind, do
all she could to cast it from her.

In her neat but scantily furnished room it was a
picture that held the place of honour. This picture
was the sketch Gifford had made of Mr. Tanaka at
the butts. Ayame never looked at this without a
wistful longing in her eyes, and she would gaze upon
it for minutes at a time. She would go to sleep with
the image of its limner flickering on her eye-lids,
and in her dreams she heard the music of his voice.
Then as she stretched forth her arms in longing to
clasp him he would vanish like a phantom of the

night and she would wake with a heart dull and
aching and with a void in it that refused to be filled.

Gifford had left her his books, and these she pored
over till their pages were familiar unto her even
beyond the windings of the streets she traversed daily

to make the scanty household purchases.   The
Odyssey was her favourite volume; she had conned
it and re-conned it till whole pages were fixed
indelibly in her memory.   She would thrill again
as she read or repeated to herself.

' And even as when the sight of land is welcome to
the swimmers, whose well-wrought ship Poseidon
hath smitten on the deep, all driven with the wind
and swelling waves, and but a remnant hath escaped
the grey sea-water and swum to the shore, and their
bodies are all crusted with the brine, and gladly
have they set foot on land and escaped an evil end ;
so welcome to her was the sight of her lord, and her
white arms she would never quite let go from his
neck.'

And then she would reach forth and take her
Koto, and while her fingers strayed over the

strings she would sadly sing the old Jacobite lilt it was the custom of the artist to croon as he plied his brush. Other songs she sung also, and the burden of each and all of them was sad and plaintive. In truth the weary days waxed long with her, and in her dreams only had she a mournful joy.

But soon her songs had to be sung without the accompaniment of the *Koto*. For Tanaka san fell sick, sick even nigh unto death, and poverty began to pinch the household shrewdly. One thing after another of the scanty furnshings had to be turned into food and medicine, and among them went the *Koto*. Soon nought was left, but the scantiest of clothing and the walls, and of credit there was none to be had more. The fish-vendor and the rice-merchant had alike refused to sell without payment, and were pressing and insistent in their claims for arrears.

The first day Ayame had been sent away empty from the rice-merchant's shop she fancied she had seen old Ishida san in the little four-and-a-half mat room behind it; however she made up her mind she must have been mistaken. For whatever could bring the old doctor so far afield to this poor quarter of the city?

With old Tanaka things were now in evil case. It was *Kakke* that had assailed him. And to combat

this disease good food, and fresh air, and foreign
wines were needful.   But how to find them, now
that even the wherewithal to fill the rice-pot was
wanting ? Not even the simplest meal was in the
house.

One thing saleable only was left.   That was
Gifford's sketch.   She went and took it down, and
looked at it with a world of sadness.

"There is no help for it! And he will never
come back, and perhaps even in time he will pass
from my life.   It was but a dream, but oh! 'twas a
dream pleasant beyond telling."

So ran the current of her unspoken thoughts.

She wrapped it up in a *furoshiki* (wrapper) and
hastened out into the lane.   She went hurriedly
pattering on past the theatres towards the little
picture-shop at the end of the street, for she was
afraid her resolution to part with the keepsake
would fail.   What a mockery the bright sunlight and
the smiling crowd hieing theatre-wards seemed to
her!

As she passed along she noticed a tall man,
on high clogs, in *hakama*, turn and look after her
curiously.   It struck her that his hair was odd ; it
curled into locks in a fashion rare in Japan.   It is
difficult to say how it was on this single fact her
mind seized, for her soul was dulled and numbed
with grief.

It was with bitter thoughts that she returned.
Sixty *sen* would not do much to prolong the agony.
For her there was but once resource left, and that

was worse than death. She looked with a shudder
at the towers and spires and vanes of the Flower
Quarter, glittering and flashing in the sunlight as if
in mockery. Already of a night she had found
herself looking out upon the soft radiance of the
electric-light streaming out from their summits,
brighter far than the gleam of the old light-house
on the spit with its kindly message of peace and

safety to forwandered wayfarers over the darkling
sea, and wondering if any fate might haply save her
from such a consummation.

To-morrow the die would be cast. She could
not let her uncle die;—her uncle who had been
even more than father and mother to her. It was
bitter, bitter for a maiden of *samurai* blood, but
many a fairer and better than she had to submit
and thole in silence, with a heart of lead and a smile
on their faces. It was her duty; and therefore if
nought else offered she would do it. For with a
Japanese maiden *ko* (filial affection) is the cardinal
virtue, to which even the chastity of the body must
be immolated when need demands. But to Ayame
the cup was more than Marah-bitter.

She was on the point of entering when she heard
voices in her uncle's room, so instead of pushing
aside the wicket of the *genka* she went round and
entered by the kitchen.

She gently slid the *karakami* apart and looked
into the room. The guest was the old Chinese
Doctor from Misaki, Ishida Shozo. She hastily
shut the *karakami* and sat down to listen. Not
without being noted by those keen old eyes however, although Ishida san seemed to have seen nothing. He had evidently just come in; for the last
words of the preliminary salutations were scarcely
done and ended.

"Ha! ha!" laughed Ishida san, "I must compliment you on the skilful way you have hidden your honourable self, for to find this house is much more difficult than to diagnose a young woman's disease. And that sometimes passes all medical skill. Ha! ha! But really those windings are very tortuous and bothersome, but at last I have found you, my old friend, although you tried to give me the slip!"

He ran on with a heartiness of good-nature which if not natural, was at all events very well assumed.

"And now," he proceeded without giving Tanaka san a chance of speaking, "how do I find you? They tell me it is *kakke* that impairs your honourable health. And you truly must have been very much troubled and inconvenienced! But I must say it was really most unkind of you not to let your old friend know of your bad circumstances. But honourably deign to let me have a humble look."

This was going ahead rather fast, and assuming a good deal, for the acquaintanceship between the twain was slight and had to climb many a degree before it put on the warm hues of friendship. Tanaka san had never been more than coldly polite to the other, but now was not the time to protest.

The doctor, gently but firmly removed the quilt, and felt and inspected the limb. His face lengthened into elongated gravity as he did so.

"And to think," he remonstrated in an injured tone, "that this honourable sickness should have attacked you so severely and you never even sent to tell me, your old friend Ishida Shozo. Not even to send one single stroke of the brush. Surely you will confess you have been unkind!"

Then changing his tone, he became professional and oracular. He poured forth a runlet of Chinese scientific terms, exactly in the manner of a mediæval tonsorial blood-letter. Then he wound up:—

"And it is medicine you must have,—such and such, and such and such, and such and such."

And he immediately whipped out his pocket-book from his bosom, and fished out from it a little heap of pills and powders which he laid on the mats beside him.

"And," he went on glibly, "a visit to the hotsprings and some *gyu-niku* (beef) and foreign wines will be good. For if this is not done, it will probably be that your honourable life will soon become extinct."

Mr. Tanaka said he was quite aware of the fact, but that inasmuch as these things could not he had, there was no help for it.

"Not to be had! Oh! Your honourable side *will* persist in teasing me. If you will deign to accept a matter of four or five hundred *yen* out of our old friendship, you will do me much honour.

Tanaka san politely but firmly told him he could not dream of such a thing.

"*Kekko! kekko!* (Admirable! admirable!)," put in the Doctor. "That is the true old *yamato-damashii* (Japanese spirit) of the Samurai, and I cannot express how much it commands my unworthy respect." (To Ayame's prejudiced ear there was a tinge of underlying irony in this.) "But what about the *o-josama* (the young lady of the house) and Santaro san?"

Through the flimsy partition Ayame heard her uncle draw a heavy breath as he set his teeth hard.

"Now then," proceeded Ishida san, "my unworthy self will venture to make a humble proposal; though it is with much dread I take the great liberty of doing so. In Kiga I have a poor *yadoya* (inn) belonging to me. It is a poor and coarse place but the hot-baths are good, and there is plenty of food and drink. If you will condescend to accept the hospitality of this broken-down hut, you will overpower me with honour. It will cost me nothing, only a trifle; merely a few *mai* per month. Because guests there are not plentiful now, there are many empty rooms."

Tanaka san thought for a moment, and then thanked him. He finally consented on the understanding that if he recovered he should discharge his obligation, counting at the rate of 40 *yen* per month for himself and Ayame. Having settled this, the old doctor made his bow with many protestations of friendship and obligation and with much sucking-in of breath.

On getting into the street he hobbled off straight to the fishmonger's and the rice-merchant's.

" If Tanaka san orders anything, send it at once and don't ask for payment,—*at present!*" he added significantly. " To do so will be good."

Then he called a *jinrikisha*, and drove off to a neighbouring *yadoya* where he found Ishida Taro awaiting him.

"As for the business, how is it?" asked the latter eagerly.

" *Domo!*" replied the old sinner. "It is much repute as a *nakodo* (middle man) that your unworthy father has already acquired, but this will be the most splendid triumph of all. It looks as if it will be good,—very good."

And he softly rubbed his parchment-like hands and chuckled to himself deep down in his throat.

IV.

It was on a lovely day in early autumn when the
S. S. *Tartaric* rounded the Susaki lighthouse on
the Bōshū coast inward bound. All her passengers
were crowding her bulwarks, binoculars in hand,
raking the coast and going into the conventional
raptures over the beauties of the landscape and
seascape. Only one appeared to be more or
less oblivious to them, and that was the Rev. Paul
Julius.

He sat on a bench not far from the deck-cabins, engaged in the agonies of metrical composition.   On a leaf of his pocket-book he had written as follows :—

I've ne'er a chick or wife or fere
Or kith or kin to bear in mind,
And oft I sigh to deem a tear
Can ne'er be claimed by aught behind.
Yet, after all, perhaps 'tis well :—
I only reap as I have sown ;
And whoso quails before the flood
That streams from letting of his own
Is not the man I'd care   .   .   .   .

   .   .   .   .

So when I think, I thank the fates
That I'm unfettered in this clime ;
Perhaps some Peri now awaits
The rhymer of this empty rhyme ;
Perhaps some girl with laughing face
And soft low voice and talking eyes
                    saving grace
Will find her joy and ~~sweet solace~~
In answering love-sick sighs with sighs.
If not, I'll reap as I have sown ;
And strongest he who stands alone.

So crush down cark and banish care,
And sombre brooding-phantasy!
To-day you sun gleams bright and fair,
Fair gleams that coast-line all alee;
Its crankling bights and sandy creeks
And scarpy swelling pine-clad hills,
And each curve of its rounded peaks
Vibrate with sharp cicadae trills;
The fair south wind shrills from the main
Nor is his pinions dank with rain.

It was all complete with the exception of the candal appendage of the first Stanza, and this want caused Mr. Julius much wrinkling of his sacerdotal forehead.

The Reverend Paul Julius was typical of the class to which it was his boast to belong. Of course there are many in the livery of the thirty-nine stripes who are manly men, and real grit from rind to core, yet the average English Curate reminds you of a Trinity of milksop, man-milliner and old woman, three persons in one, the same in substance, and equal in power and glory. In the case of the Rev. Paul the combination was set off with a beneficent simper that much rehearsing had rendered natural and constantly abiding. And besides a rapt seraphic look seemed to wait for ever on his beck and call, ready to swim up into his clear and stag-like eyes and suffuse them with a luminous haze that reminded you of the halo in a picture of the Madonna. It was expressive of piety, of resignation, and of unspeakable sympathy with all kinds of sorrow from sudden bereavement down to the cholic, and of lots of other things too numerous to inventory. When he would press the knob and summon up this look as he pensively filled up a meerschaum as black as the smoke-stack of the steamer with Lovejack, the effect was fine although not perhaps so pathetic as he meant it to be. His seeming then for all the world was that of a cherub trying to look at once comical and saintly. And it was not once or twice a day that he presented that semblance, for the meerschaum was constantly either in his hands or in his mouth. He appeared to lay it aside only at meal times and at prayers.

After the prayers had been negotiated to the unqualified satisfaction of the missionary ladies on board he would invariably stray towards the smoking-room. Here he would sit and listen to stories such as are wont to be retailed in that quarter, smiling deprecation not unmingled with a smirk at anything savouring of the *risqué*. Nor was he above diluting the dryness of doctrinal discussion with whiskey and soda—in moderation of course.

But in spite of all this he was not exactly popular with the males among his fellow-pas-

sengers to start with. By the officers and the
ship's company generally, he came very near being
held in horror if not in detestation.

To commence proceedings he had come on board
in a seemingly very casual way, and without ever
so much as saying by your leave, had told the
purser that 'his ship looked a very fine vessel, and
that after an inspection to make sure that looks
squared with reality he *might* possibly take a
passage in her. Of course he expected the very
best cabin,—one where there would be none of 'that
very painful and trying sea-sickness.'

He then went off on his tour of inspection. It
seemed to range pretty well all over the boat
from stem to stern. He had poked his nose
into the Ladies' cabin and was only repelled by
a shrill shriek of dismay. It came from behind a
something white that looked like a sheet or a —
garment hastily raised in front of his prying eyes.
Then with a mellifluous apology, given with deliber-
ation and a soupçon of an Irish brogue, he slowly retreated to the officer's quarters. He religiously sniffed
into each and all of their bunks. Next he hied him to
the cook's galley and from there through the foc'sle,
where such of the ship's company as he met
saluted his retreating hinder-parts with rude but
expressive pantomime and unsacerdotal language.
Then he had gone down into the hold, and was just

on the point of descending among the nether fires of the engine-room when the vessel cast loose and the screw began to churn the water.

"Now then, sir!" said a sharp voice behind him. "I'm afraid you haven't much choice left *now*. I hope the inspection has been satisfactory. Where shall I book you for,—Yokohama, or Honkong?"

Such had been the manner of the coming on board of the Rev. Paul Julius.

Next day his curiosity seemed to be still unsated. In spite of the notice on the brass-plate to the contrary, he had climbed with tottering steps and fluttering coat-tails on the officers' holy of holies, the bridge, and had been as a matter of course politely but firmly ejected therefrom. He regained the deck in time to see the gold-bands on the 2nd Steward's cap descending into the abyss of the ice-room. He immediately thought good to follow, and in spite of the freezing temperature he had insisted on prying into every corner and bringing his eye-glass to bear upon the quality of the meat. And all that day, and parts of the following day he made this searching and exploring his pastime. Hence it came to pass that when the ship's company spoke of his reverence they always named his profession with an adjective prefixed.

On the third day he began to devote himself to the ladies. He was not long in winning their regard. For a more dutiful squire of dames never donned Churchman's Cassock. He drank tea with them and handed round the bread and butter, he fetched them their parasols when the sun came out and their wraps when the night-breeze sprang up, he moralized with them on the wickedness and the frailty of man, and the vanity of all things, and he amused them with parlour conundrums.

But all that was nothing to the beautiful and saintly verses he wrote in their autograph albums. This was the consideration that put the finishing stroke to his popularity with the ladies.

So one evening when the 2nd officer swore he had actually seen that adjective parson with his arm round the waist of one of the missionary girls, as the twain of them stood looking over the taffrail, no one ventured to say he was mistaken. For missionary girls are but human flesh and blood after all, and often very pretty, and this parson certainly had charming ways with women.

But there were fair ones other than missionaries on board the *Tartaric* this trip. Among them was a Japanese lady of apparently some one or two and twenty summers. She had just completed her course at Vassar college, it was generally understood, and was returning to the Land of the Rising Sun as a Sweet Girl Graduate.

She travelled all alone and unprotected, but there
was not an unmarried man on the ship who would
not have been delighted to repair that oversight
on the part of Providence.

'And no wonder either.   For apart from her
considered as a compendium of erudition, Miss Tomoye was fetching in her womanliness.   Although
of a trifle over the stature of the average Japanese
woman she was slightly *petite* from an Occidental
point of view.   But yet her proportions and
symmetry were so fine that this scarcely struck
one as a fault.   Besides she appeared to be
at once firm and lithe.   When she tripped up
the companion-way holding her dress aside, she
disclosed an ankle that was really good for one's
eyes to look upon.   And then as she walked the
deck in her close-fitting bodice and skirts draped
gracefully round her,—not at all as is wont to be the
way with European skirts on a Japanese lady—
and coal-black locks straying from under the most
natty and coquettish of bonnets, she made a picture
in motion that focussed all eyes on the ship.

She was pretty, decidedly ; and although no doubt
she knew it, she was careful not to give any
sign of her consciousness of the fact.   She answered simply but shortly when spoken to, and
in the main kept herself very much to herself.
Nearly all the bachelors, and eke some of the

benedicts if the unadorned truth needs must be
spoken had tried to make themselves agreeable
to her. They got but scant reward for their pains,
—that is all with but one exception, and that exception was the adjective parson.

That worthy man had had several *tête à-têtes* with
Miss Tomoye, and the Rev. Paul had got so far
as to volunteer to write a poem for her album.
When she said she did not have any album he
said he would give her a copy of verses all the
same.

So here he stood, ransacking his brain for ideas
and his memory for rhymes, which as before intimated, had refused to accomodate him at the end
of his first stanza. He had gone on with the two
succeeding and finished them off to his own huge
satisfaction. But the conclusion of the first;—there
was the rub. He smote his forehead with his fist,
he looked up pensively at the mainmast swaying
gently as the vessel throbbed onward with the
breeze whistling among the shrouds, but come
those last lines would not.

He turned into his cabin to look up the collection
of rhymes he had made and kept in readiness to fall
back upon on an emergency of this sort. As he
was fingering his sheets uneasily, his eye caught the
whisk of the flounce of a dress he recognised at a
flash as it passed his door. He dropped his leaves,

and peered out cautiously and with much circum-
spection.

Miss Tomoye had glided up to his pocket-
book. She looked at it for a moment with a roguish
smile gradually running the circuit of her eyes
and her dimples. Then she took up his pencil,
and thinking for a minute or so, hastily scribbled
something in the volume, cast a hurried glance
around her and tripped away.

The Rev. Paul waited till she had disappeared,
and then drawing a long breath, jumped out and
pounced upon the pocket-book as a hawk darts upon
a chicken.

He gave a great gasp, when he saw that his
poem was complete. He looked at the conclusion of his first stanza with amazement that almost
amounted to consternation and which was comical
in the extreme. He read out as follows :—

> I've ne'er a chick or wife or fere
> Or kith or kin to bear in mind,
> And oft I sigh to deem a tear
> Can ne'er be claimed by aught behind.
> Yet, after all, perhaps 'tis well :—
> I only reap as I have sown ;
> And whoso quails before the flood
> That streams from letting of his own
> Is not the man I'd care " one shred
> To see my mother's daughter wed."

" Well, that's a hint tu spake out, if ever there
was wan!" he muttered to himself! " Ow the
purty darlint! she ————"

Here he stopped abruptly as if struck by paralysis.

He ran his fingers through his hair, and, as if
seized with some new and startling idea, he snatched
up his pocket-book and hastily began to rummage
in one of its numerous and over-laden compartments.
He took out an old letter torn into four or five
pieces and carefully spread them out cheek by jowl
with the two lines just so strangely added.

" The 's' and the 'd''s and the 'r''s and all of
thim the same, an' as loike as two peas in a pod,
—a perfect colliction av twins!"

Then in most unclerical language he added.

" Oh the Divil! Blazes take him, but it's a 'cute
baste he is!''

Then after another pause in which a look that
meant unutterable things gradually took possession
of his face, he muttered ;—

" An' tu think av the luvely doings wid that
ruffian in the Ladies' cabin! If it ever gets known,
thim pore missionary gurls ûll be glad av an earthquake tu help thim tu hide their blushes!"

IV.

From a European point of view Miyanoshita is the centre of civilization in the Hakone district, and the Fujiya Hotel is the Hub of that particular microcosmic universe.

Now the Fujiya is in many ways an excellent place. The rooms are comfortable, and the plenishings for the inner man are all that can be desired. The beds have a considerable amount of elasticity,—so much in fact that if you jump into them recklessly and without due caution aforethought you fancy perforce that you have fallen on the vent of a powerful artesian well.

But the waitresses are objectionable. They are, for Japanese waitresses, unconscionably pert and impudent. They have mastered the English numerals almost up to twenty, they know stray syllables of the names of most European dishes; one of them has actually got so far as to be able to say "tank you for nothing;" and when you smile and bring out your politest Japanese, they look at you with ironical self-depreciation and tell you with subtle mockery "*Eigo wo wakarimasen.*"

Now this is exasperating, for with the single exception of these saucy hussies there is scarcely a *nesan* in the country whom you can't fetch incontinently with a plentiful sprinkling of *o*'s and *go*'s and *masu*'s and the other frills of full-dress Nihongo. All this is merely another modern instance going to shew the harm of bestowing the outlines of a liberal education on the lower classes. It ruins and perverts them utterly.

But that is not to the point.

About half-a-mile beyond the Fujiya you strike a notice-board adorned with a legend. Like an old Greek manuscript it is slightly defective in the matter of punctuation and stops, but if you have the courage to wrestle with it for a minute or two, you will see that it means something. Without

counting the scrabble of hieroglyphics that frills off
its bottom, it is as follows :—

NOTICE.

*To let the tea-house Miharashi where the view is
most picture-sque looking over Kiga and nice clean
brook.*

You take the hint and make your way upward
through a darksome wood of cryptomerias. Just
as you have made up your mind that you are climb-
ing into the bowels of nowhere you come out on a
tea-house with a tiny platform perched on the edge
of a scarp. If you are wise, you will accept the old

lady's invitation to 'do an honourable bending of the loins', in order to recover your breath and to take it all in.

For in truth the prospect is pretty; in sooth the legend hath lied not;—the scene *is* really ' picturesque.'

You find yourself on the middle slope of an amphitheatre of green. If the time of your happening upon the spot be late in autumn it's uppermost circuit will be a dun rat-colour, and the whole expanse roofed in with a canopy of blue flecked with trails of fleecy white. With some levelling in the centre, a certain amount of cutting in the sides, and a few other improvements, which a Yankee contractor would do cheaply and yet make money out of the job, the place would be an ideal one for a Roman holiday, and sizeable enough to seat the whole worthless spawn of the dregs of Romulus, assembled for one of their gentle throat-cutting functions.

But it is better as it is, with its irregular clefts, its grass-clad rifts and hollows and its wintry forest of *keyaki* straggling in its scraggy leaflessness upward to its waist from the light green of its lower vegetable patches and feathery bamboo brakes. Adown it comes the Haya-kawa, tumbling over its boulders into swirls of yeasty foam and pools the colour of milk that has just been to the pump, and roaring upwards with the ceaseless crash of ocean rollers on a sandy beach some miles away. Right below our perch, just above the point where the bamboo-covered sweep thrusts the torrent against the cliff nestles the little hamlet of Kiga.

It consists of not more than a score of houses, and almost every one of these without exception is a 'hotel.' The great attraction of the spot lies in its waters ; they are the most celebrated of those in the neighbourhood.

Now one of these ' hotels ' was the establishment Ishida Sho-zo had referred to as "his broken-down establishment," and to it after a weary day's jolting Tanaka san, and Ayame found their way.

The change of environment soon

began to tell on the *kakke*, for the old quack's pills and potions were harmless, and the waters of his hotel were potent. Besides they have good cooks in Kiga.

Wherefore Mr. Tanaka recovered apace, much to Ayame's rejoicing, although she sighed when she thought of a settling of accounts. For instinct told her that she would have to pay the score.

So one morning shortly after her uncle had again set foot on the ground, she was not at all astonished to learn that Ishida Shozo had once more come a-wooing. Her uncle merely intimated the fact to her casually, but she knew well that it was a matter of grave anxiety to him, and occupied his mind during most of his waking hours. When he spoke of it she appeared to take no notice, only uttering an apparently careless '*Sō desu ka?*' But half-an-hour later she hied her forth and climbed the mountain-path to be alone and to think. She sat her down on the platform in front of Miharashi and thanking the old woman for the tea she brought her, told her that she wished to be alone for a time.

She sat gazing down below, but seeing nothing, or seeing what she did see all blurred, or as if in a dream,—a dream that ever would revert to the villa on the cliff, the lighthouse with its kindly gleam, the old gnarled pine-tree by the path and to what was said under it one evening away back in May, now seemingly ages ago. In spite of herself her thoughts would stray waywardly thither, although she tried to stifle them with a strong and merciless hand. The very roar of the torrent called up the crash of the sea when the winds blew strong, and the waves ran high ; and when she thought of the sea, she———— .

Just at that moment she heard voices, and the 'click, clack' of wooden *geta* in the courtyard behind. In a moment the speakers were upon her. She looked up quickly with a flush, for in her tense and high-strung nervous state she fancied they must have overheard her thoughts, although in truth she had never moved her lips.

It was a man and a woman; both evidently of high rank. This was nothing to be wondered at, for the roofs of Kiga often shelter a largeish section of the Peerage of Japan. The man—they both were Japanese—was in European clothes, and wore them as if he had never worn anything else. What a contrast he presented to Ishida Taro ! she thought, as her eye travelled rapidly over him. He was young, apparently not more than five or six and twenty, possibly not so much as that, and certainly junior to the lady that accompanied him.

As they came forward to the platform, and with many apologies for disturbing her, took their seats opposite to Ayame, she allowed her eyes to travel over the woman with much curiosity. From her tortoise-shell hair pins to her lacquered *geta* with their dainty velvet toe-straps, there was nothing but faultless taste. Her pose, her manners, her hands and the way she used them all argued high breeding and refinement. Her face was a fine one, with its rose-bud like mouth, its long straight nose, and its symmetrical oval sweep. But the eyes were its striking feature ; when she talked they would light up and sparkle like stars when the frost is hanging in the sky. Ayame fancied she had seen her somewhere before but she could not recall the occasion. She put away the idea as a hallucination.

After the old woman had brought tea and sweetmeats, the lady again turned and addressed herself to Ayame. The language she used was of the most stately and ceremonious order, and was uttered in a tone that was music itself. In talking with her Ayame forgot her troubles ; her coming was as a ray of sunshine in the morning.

At last they rose and walked together to the bottom of the path. Ayame went into the hotel, and the other twain fared onward towards the Otometoge.

That evening as the light fell Ayame took a *koto* and began to play. The songs she sang were sad and mournful, for her heart was heavy. When she stopped and rose to shut the *shoji*, she saw that she had

had an audience. Her friends of the morning were standing in the middle of the road-way listening.

This had been early in October. One day a fortnight later, Ishida Shozo had paid another visit to his hotel, and the following morning Mr. Tanaka opened to Ayame the purport of his coming.

It was a bitter half-hour that followed, although Ayame had foreseen this ending from afar. She merely bowed her head, and said that if such was Ishida san's honourable request and her uncle's honourable wish she would obey.

That evening Ishida Shozo carried back the tidings to Tokyo. After he had related in full how his tactics had prospered, he knocked out the ashes from his *kiseru* on the *hibachi*, and laying it down beside him he rubbed his skinny palms together with huge satisfaction.

" *Sō sa!* " he broke out. " It is good for the poor *isha sama* (doctor) to bring down the old-time *samurai* pride. It is good, very good!"

V.

Under the special circumstances of the case, there had been no ceremony of *mi-ai* (mutual seeing) in the courtship of Ayame and Ishida Taro. But in November the *yuinō* (betrothal) took place with all due formality.

It only remained to choose the 'lucky day.' In this matter Mr. Ishida's convenience was consulted. For Mr. Ishida was now, or at least purported to be, a very busy man. The First Japanese Legislative Furnace was now in full blast, and Ishida Taro was supposed to be helping to blow the bellows. The Diet had been opened with state and ceremony, and the two Houses, an Upper and a Lower, had addressed themselves to their work. In the case of the Upper this meant in the main honest and capable legislation. In the case of the Lower it was something different and much simpler. To the majority of the 300 chosen Representatives of a fifteen *yen* tax-paying people it seemed that their duties were twofold. In the first place they had all to try and speak at once, and in the second they had to cut down everybody's salary except their own. And in these laudable endeavours Mr. Ishida Taro had to do his three-hundredth share of the task, otherwise his constituents might make nasty remarks.

Therefore the marriage was to be deferred to the New Year's Recess, when the fiction is that all men, legislators included, repose from their labours.

Mr. Ishida, notwithstanding the arduous nature of his Parliamentary toils, yet found time to make odd flying visits to Miyanoshita. There he had made the acquaintance of a Mr. Furukawa, with whom it soon became his delight to consort. For Mr. Furukawa, besides being a very pleasant and and stylish gentleman had passed many years of his life in foreign lands. He had read Mill's 'Political Economy' and Spencer's 'Study of Sociology,' and that in Mr. Ishida's eyes was no small title to respect. For although Mill and Spencer are to the advanced politician of the West interesting mainly as relics of an exploded system of sociology they are names to swear by in the case of not a few Japanese philosophers. Wherefore it was the wont of Ishida Taro to repair to the Naraya Hotel for a weekly dose of inspiration.

Since their first meeting at Miharashi, Ayame had seen Mr. Furukawa several times, and his 'honorable companion' oftener. For Ayame had found out that she was not his wife. She was Kotake, one of the most famous among the *geisha* of the Capital. When she was told this, Ayame recollected where she had seen her face before; it had been in a zincograph supplement to one of the smaller newspapers that find their *metier* in chronicling the life, and sayings, and doings and eke the scandals of the Japanese Hetairae.

Kotake would often come up to Ayame's hotel' and the two women would sit together on the verandah feeding the great lazy *koi* and gold fish that basked beneath the waters of the fountains that splashed into their pools. In the course of these half-hours the women talked of many things. From looks and hints and occasional meaning words, Ayame was not slow to perceive that Kotake knew how it stood with her, and that she was aware she was in evil case. As the days went by, the elder woman ventured to speak plainly and yet more plainly and one day she opened all her mind to the girl.

It was at a tea-house beyond the Otome-toge.

There Ayame had gone to be alone and to think,
meaning to pass the night there and to return next
forenoon. About half-past four she heard *jinrikisha*
drive up and Mr. Furukawa and Kotake appeared.
Kotake alighted and came into the inn while Furukawa san went on further into the village. Kotake
had seen Ayame and came and greeted her.

Then after some bantering talk she asked her
plainly if she would not like to become a Geisha.

"A Geisha!" said Ayame with surprise. "That
needs much training, and many accomplishments.
And then my uncle says the life is not an honourable
one—at least not now."

"Our life not honoured!" interrupted the other,
flashing up. "Yes, there are people who say so.
But there are also people who say what a fine thing
it is to be a teacher and how honourable is the work
of training the minds of the young. And yet if one
asks 'What has become of my old friend Mr.
So and So? and is told that he has become a teacher
in a *jinjō shōgakko* (elementary school) or even in
a *chūgakko* (middle school) what is said and done?
Do they not mutter '*So desu ka?*' (Is that so?) in a
tone of pity, shrug their shoulders, and change
the subject, not wishing to sadden each other by
talking of a social wreck? And yet newspapers
write lectures about teachers' noble work, governors
and officers make speeches about it and Ministers

of the Cabinet and Foreign Representatives read
addresses about it at meetings of the Educational
Society. And what does it all mean? Nothing!
All the time these honourable gentlemen are all
laughing in their sleeves. But it is the right thing
to talk as they do, and they do it."

She stretched out a shapely arm towards the
hibachi and knocked out the ashes from her pipe.
Then meditatively rolling a fresh pill of tobacco
and pressing it into the tiny bowl of the silver-
mounted *kiseru* she leant forward and lit it at the
live charcoal. She took two or three whiffs, inhaling
the smoke, and then opening her little mouth she
allowed it to stream out in filmy wreaths and spirals.

"And with us now," she resumed, looking
curiously at the smoke as it faded into space. "how
is it? Just the very reverse. People pretend
to despise us; but do they? Honourable and
learned Professors of the University attack us and
say we are despicable, and folks listen to them approvingly and say they are honourably right. But
when people leave the lecture-hall they think they
have been very good to listen to such dry de-
liverances and that their virtue really is entitled to
a reward. So they go to a tea-house and call for
us, and we go, and they tell us all about it and the
learned Professor's argument becomes the seed of
many amusing things."

She laughed a quiet little laugh, vibrating with scornful contempt.

"See there!" she said suddenly pointing to the bridge in front of the other wing of the building. "You see that honourable young lady with the sunshade. Well, she is a teacher, and she works six hours a day. And what does she receive for her labour? You see her *obi*;—it is not very handsome, and yet it means two months of her salary. My own insignificant and coarse one is better and more tasteful and would cost twice as much, and yet I could earn it in two evenings. Then what lies before the honourable female-teacher? I will tell you. She will marry some small officer, or some farmer, or some merchant with a little shop and in five and twenty years from now she will be exactly like that *oba-san* (old lady) on the mats up in the corner. Surely it is much honour and benefit she derives from the honourable praises of her profession in the newspapers, at lectures, and even from the *Mombu-daijin* (Minister for Education) and the honourable Professors of the University."

Ayame said that in Japan woman was weak, but that in foreign countries she was not so.

"Yes" replied Kotake san. "It is so. I heard the honourable Count Aruhito say one evening to a foreign guest he had invited;—"When I marry,

I get an upper servant; when *you* marry, you become an upper servant!"

"But was not Countess Aruhito formerly a *geisha?*"

"Yes, she had the honour to be so!" replied Kotake san with a meaning smile, " And so was the Countess Tamanaga, and the Baroness Sakurada, and several other of the honourable wives of the nobles and statesmen. My unworthy self might now be the Marchioness This, or the Viscountess That, if I had chosen. But I prefer to be simply Kotake of the Nakamuraya of Shimbashi, and independent. For we alone among Japanese women are our own mistresses."

Ayame said something that implied very delicately and indirectly that report ran to the effect that they were sometimes the mistresses of other people as well, for the knowledge of such a fact is not all inconsistent with modesty on the part of a Japanese maiden.

Kotake san merely shrugged her shoulders, and re-arranged her long robes under her knees.

"It may be so," she replied at last. "But such a thing is only necessary on the part of those whose accomplishments begin and end with a beautiful face. That alone has made many a fortune; I do not pretend to deny it. There is at present my honourable friend O Kiku

san," (this with a tinge of irony), "for example.
She was the wife of a small shop-keeper, and got
divorced, and joined a house in Shimbashi. And
although she could neither play nor sing, and although she was without art and totally uneducated,
she is now called by the newspapers the Chrysan-
themum Bank, because she is so rich. But she had
a pretty face. But with all women it is not so."

She stopped to punctuate her discourse with the
kiseru (pipe) on the *hibachi*. After she had refilled
its tiny bowl she went on.

"But that is a shameful thing, and we are not
proud of O-kiku san and such as she. A woman
with accomplishments need never do as she does,

The tongue of a clever woman is as a two-edged sword. If she uses it aright no one will take liberties with her honourable person. These fingers of mine are small and slight" (here she laid down her pipe and stretched out her hands, and dainty indeed they were with their flashing finger-rings), "but" she added slowly "they are more powerful than Benkei's. They more than once have held a Minister's fate within their grasp, and when I *have* closed them . . . . ."

She stopped abruptly with an aposiopesis eloquent of an unspoken catastrophe.

"But," put in Ayame, "surely such is not the case with many singers of these times?"

Kotake san's mobile lips were again wreathed with a smile. It spelled power, superiority, complacency and many other things besides, all in a monosyllable.

"No!" she answered. "You are augustly right. But I am Kotake of the Nakamuraya. And as for my unworthy side in my day I have done even more brilliant things than my friend, O Haru san of Asakusa."

"As for her famous exploit, what may it be?" asked Ayame with some curiosity.

"Can it really be that you have not heard,— you who are to become the honourable wife of a member of our august Diet. Surely, surely it is

strange! But the story is an amusing one. O Haru
san had a sweetheart, a newspaper man, who was
studying law at the University. And his Professor
heard of his love for her, and reproved him, and
at last had him driven out from the college.
Then when the elections came on, the august *sensei*
stood for Asakusa. And then O Haru san told
Kobayashi san, her sweetheart, to oppose him.
Now Asakusa Ku is a poor place ; only in it the Yoshiwara is rich. Most of the electors are the land-
lords of the houses in that quarter. And O Haru
san knew them all and was very popular with them.
So she went round and told them the story, and
they all voted for her sweetheart, and he won, and
now she says he must go on the Budget Committee
and vote for cutting down the salary of the honourable Professor who chased him out of the University."

She wound up with a few more vigorous punctuation marks on the metal-rim of the brazier.

"But I am really a chatter-box, and have not yet
made a beginning of what I wanted to say. My unworthy side has a humble proposal to make to you.
I am now getting to be an *Oba-san* (old woman) and
am not so active as I was. And although my awkward
house is a small one, it has been famous from long
ago. And I am anxious to have a clever woman to
take my place when I become too old for men to

call me any longer. There are one *geisha*, and two *Oshaku* (dancing-girls) in it, but their understanding is not so quick. Now I have often heard you playing the *koto* and the *shamisen*, and singing, and you are really skillful, and soon you would easily become more so. Besides you have read many books, and—you must not think I am *oseji-mono* (a flatterer)—you are clever and talk with cunning and understanding. Besides, as for foreign tongues, you know the English, and among geisha as far as this goes, you will be *mezurashii mono* (a rarity), and Japanese are always fond of *mezurashii mono*. Now, as to coming to my house, how is it? What do you say?"

"You overwhelm me with your kindness," replied Ayame after an astonished pause " but it is impossible."

Kotake san's quick ear caught the regret underlying the tone of the refusal.

" Is it because you are to wed an honourable member of the Diet that you refuse? I humbly beg you to consider. It will be penny wise and pound foolish. According to the proverb, 'the great man has no seed,' and this is true of Ishida Shozo, although he is not a great man, but only a cunning old fox. Both of them, father and son, I know well, because both of them have often called me. They are both often the guests of the singers. The honour-

able member of the Diet has no wits; he is only a glib
share-mono (dandy.)   He will never be a famous
man, and because he will be disappointed he will be
severe to his wife.   Excuse me, if I give you pain,
but I know it well."

"Oh!" said Ayame.   "I am very much obliged
to you for the kind interest you take in me.   But
please stop.   There are circumstances which I cannot . . . . . ."

As Ayame came to an abrupt stop Kotake san
looked at her closely.

"I thought it would be so.   But if ever things go
ill with you, and you think better of my humble
proposal, remember!   A matter of 500 *mai* will
easily be arranged for clothes and hair-pins and an
obi for you.   But excuse me for pressing you.   I
think I will honourably do my leave-taking.   I see
that the honourable master has returned."

As she rose to go she caught Ayame's questioning look.

"As for this honourable master, you seem to ask
who he is.   Well, a hard-working *geisha* must take
a little leisure and amuse herself occasionally.   And
this honourable master pays me three hundred *mai*
for a month's holiday at the hot-springs.   But he
can afford it, for he seems to be as rich as *Yebisu*
(the Japanese Plutus) himself.   And he is also very
amusing, for he has just returned from foreign

countries where he has been since the time he was
small.   He has many delightful stories to tell, and
a talkative old woman like me likes amusing stories,
because it is with them she pleases the honourable
guests who call her.   But pray excuse me, for I
must be going,"

Again she bowed low, and Ayame was left alone
with her thoughts.   And her thoughts were troubled
ones.

"Why did I not meet her two months ago?"
ran the refrain of the wild chorus of agony that rang
in her ears.   "If on that night when I sold the
picture I had but seen her! Alas! alas!"

Then she sank forward, and while her hands
pressed her head she rapidly revolved one thing
after another in her mind.

Oh! to stop it all, what happiness! But it was
not to be thought of.   Her uncle's word had been
given, and that ended the matter.   To break it
causelessly would be disgrace, and to him disgrace
was worse than death.   No! No! But it *was*
cruel.

She sat for long, looking out through the opened
shojis that gave on the wheat-fields behind the
house.   The prospect over them was a cheerless
one; they were bleak and raw with an unkindly
wind whistling across their sodden expanse beard-
ed with drills and clumps of *mugi*, all a-shiver for

their swathing of protecting snow.   As the breeze
soughed through the fringe of stunted pines that
barred the lower horizon, the trees seemed to nod
and wave at her in impish mockery.   Away beyond
was the dull mist-rack of afternoon slowly lapping
the flanks of Fuji with its oozy, fleecy haze.   It was
slowly creeping up towards his shoulders and summit, which grim, and gaunt, and massive, and with
the first snows of the season flecking and streaking
the topmost slopes, seemed to lower and gloom
upon the world below like the creature of nightmare.   As she gazed aloft, Ayame told herself that

in yet two months he would be clothed in one great robe of shimmering white, and that then she too would clothe herself all in white, and at nightfall old Ishida Shozo and his wife would come to bear her away to what was colder and more hateful than the tomb.

With these and kindred thoughts she sat on until gloaming thickened around her. And then, as if with the rush of a torrent that may not be stemmed, it came into her mind how sweetly one evening four month's before the dusk had thickened around her on the cliffs as she had stood hand in hand with him that had come into her life unknown and perforce, and watched the lights flash out their helpful message to the ships.

It was too heavy for her to bear; she arose and shut the *shojis* with a shudder. To her it seemed like locking the gates of heaven behind herself, for that memory of the past had to be done to death without pity or ruth.

VI.

Early in December Kotake vanished from Miyanoshita and Ayame saw her no more in Kiga.
There had been a misunderstanding in the Furukawa establishment, and the head thereof had waxed
wroth and warm, and had indulged in the luxury of
strong language. He had sent his 'honourable

companion ' off to her room quaking, as he fancied. But Kotake was like John Knox in one point—she never had feared the face of man.

So when she reappeared on the scene fifteen minutes later to humbly apologise, as Furukawa san supposed, she astonished him by telling him with mock ceremony that ' by his kind shade she would do an honourable leave-taking.'

Whereupon Mr. Furukawa began to do the apologising. Kotake took it all as a matter of course, told him with a queenly air not to mention it, and then proceeded to treat him to such a stinging tongue-lashing as only a *geisha* among Japanese women can administer. Then as he stood there flushing and helpless, she walked down-stairs where two *kuruma* laden with luggage and an empty one awaited her, got into the unoccupied vehicle, and gave the signal for the procession to proceed.

As she wound round the curves of the downward grade, Kotake summed up the spoils of her autumn campaign. They amounted to 600 *yen* in bank-notes, sundry rings and other trinkets in the matter of jewelry, and *a secret,*—for Furukawa san was addicted to speaking in his sleep.

Mr. Furukawa still stayed on at Naraya's, although the place was getting dull. He made one or two short visits to Tokyo whence he usually returned with Ishida Taro. But in spite of this, time was beginning to hang heavily on his hands. He seemed to welcome even mild distractions.

One of his latest sources of amusement was a new coolie, that had been engaged by the hotel about a week after Kotake's going. He was comical to behold, and Furukawa found him comical in his talk and in his notions when he got on speaking terms with him, as he soon did. For Kichibei was a bundle of contradictions. He kept to the old Japanese tonsure, of a shaven furrow running along the ridge of his head, and an old percussion gun-hammer top-knot, and that although his hair, contrary to use and wont, showed a natural inclination to run into curls. And yet Kichibei was endeavouring to cultivate a moustache with no mean measure of success. His eyes which were Mongolian to a degree, seemed literally adance with fun and laughter. And Furukawa san found his mental garnishings to be a mass of topsy-turveydom gorgeous more by far than the stage of Drury Lane at Pantomime season. Wherefore Mr. Furukawa delighted in Kichibei, for Mr. Furukawa had a keen sense of humour.

For some little time he confined his efforts to exploiting Kichibei's notions on things in general. But by and by he gave Kichibei to understand that *he* had passed most of his time in foreign parts. At this statement Kichibei dropped the hoe he was wielding, and turned round to him with a face on which holy reverence and respect was writ in large text capitals.

" *Na-ru-ho-do!* " he gasped.

Then Furukawa san began to expatiate on foreign manners and customs. Kichibei's quaint comments thereon simply sent him into roars. And when the coolie took to plying him with questions, Mr. Furukawa's amusement was, if anything, redoubled. For the queries were posers that called for answers worthy of the occasion, and the traveller did his best to rise to it.

A week went past and Furukawa felt that Kichibei was still far from being worked out. Therefore, whenever he wanted anything done, it was Kichibei that was summoned for the service.

So one Saturday in the middle of December, when he and Ishida, who had run up from Tokyo, made up their minds for an excursion, it was Kichibei who was entrusted with charge of the commissiriat. He was called into the room where the twain were sitting talking. As he entered, Furukawa san wound up :—

"And so although she has not Kotake's style perhaps, still she hasn't got Kotake's tongue and Kotake's temper. Yes! I think that buying O Kiku san will be good!"

Then he stopped abruptly, and turned round to

where Kichibei stood smiling and bowing and ducking.

"Because it is fine weather to-day," Furukawa began, "and we are going to Ojigoku for the sake of exercise, condescend, hastening, to prepare luncheon portions for two men."

When an order is given by a Japanese even to a coolie, it is always garnished with a preamble of explanations.

"*He! He!* I do a humble consent. As for wine, what shall I cause to be taken along?"

"As for wine, two bottles of beer, a bottle of whiskey, and two bottles of soda-water will do."

Kichibei, said "*He! He! Kashikomarimashita,*" ducked, and retired with a grin running from ear to ear.

"A whole bottle of whiskey!" he said to himself. "*Naruhodo!* That is good!"

In half-an-hour they were all under way, toiling up the ascent past Sokokura and through Ni-no-taira.

Ojigoku is not a very charming spot, and the way to it is not pleasant for tender feet. The guide-book says the aspect of the scene is wild and desolate and the guide-book tells the truth. The place *is* wild and fearsome, with fire, and boiling-water, and swirling steam, and brimstone stench enough to furnish forth two very decent old-fashioned Presbyterian Hells. The Big Hell *is* really the name the Japanese used to give it, but that has been officially changed to O-waki-dani, or the valley of the greater boiling. But the re-christening of the place has not had any very appreciable effect upon its looks. It is still as ugly and gruesome as ever.

Furthermore, the guide-book is authority for the statement that 'the footing is insecure in many places, and fatal accidents have occurred both to Japanese and foreigners.' In this respect also its words are sooth. A few days before Furukawa san's pic-nic, an unfortunate fire-wood cutter had fallen through its crust and had been as good as turned into soup. The funeral of his remains had passed Mr. Furukawa's window on the day following the event.

Now, impelled by morbid curiosity, Mr. Furukawa drew over-close to the scene of the mishap. Ishida san protested, and the coolie spoke volubly of the danger. But Mr. Furukawa being a man of will, and not deficient in courage, and somewhat fond of letting the world at large know the fact, would insist on advancing.

"Why," he laughed scornfully. "A shark once tried to swallow me, but he found it difficult. And this is not half so lively as the shark!"

Ishida said nothing, but the coolie muttered

something under his breath, and then wound up with
a Dominic Sampson "*Naruhodo!*" uttered in an
awe-struck confidential whisper that might have
been heard three hundred yards away.

Furukawa san picked his way onward. When
at the lip of the hole whence the steam came hiss-
ing in spurts and jets, he turned and looked over
his shoulder with a smile of scornful contempt on
his face. Suddenly he tottered, and the smile gave
way to a look of absolute funk and fright. At the
same time, right behind him, the ground gave way
with a wheeze, and a gush of water and vapour
hid him from sight.

Ishida san simply stood quaking and shaking
in his traces, without even the power to run
away, which as likely as not was his natural
inclination. But the coolie threw down his load,
and with an exclamation that sounded uncommonly
like 'D—— n it all,' sprang round the newly opened vent, and dashing into the steam, dragged out
the venturesome Furukawa by main force and the
collar.

Furukawa lay for some time gasping and panting
and then he got up laughing a jarring uneasy laugh.

"That was a slightly dangerous thing," he said,
making light of it. "As for you" (this to the coolie)
"it was very kind and brave of you, but there was no
need to risk yourself. I was coming out myself."

The coolie bowed low, and humbly begged pardon for his offence. But there was a curious flicker in his eyes as he raised his head. Ishida san came forward to support Mr. Furukawa's view of the matter.

"As for you," he said turning to the *ninsoku* (coolie), "do you understand English?"

The coolie again bowed humbly, and once more begged pardon for this second offence.

"I once was on an English ship," he went on to explain with much circumlocution, "and that is all I learned. It was what the foreigners said when they were excited!"

They set forward, passed Ubago, and came down upon the lake at Ume-jiri. It was there that they proposed to lunch. So the coolie set down his burden and opened the baskets. The friends set to work upon the eatables, not neglecting the liquid comforts the *ninsoku* had uncorked for them. He, being a man of far more than normal activity, fashioned a bamboo into a fishing-rod, and fixing a hook on a piece of line he had brought with him began to tempt the fishes.

The day was clear and crisp and cold, and the two friends made good progress with the whiskey. The coolie looked round, and noted with a leer in his eye that the bottle was half-empty and that none of its contents had been spilled either. From where

he was he could catch their words quite easily, for
although their talk was passing amicable and con-
fidental, its tone was pitched in no minor key.
They were speaking in English,—Furukawa with
glib correctness, and the other with many stumbles
and falls over words as big as Pre-Adamite boulders.

"Hush!" broke in Mr. Furukawa. "The *ninsoku* seems to be listening."

"Well, that is not of significance," replied Ishida
airily. "He only knows sailor's oaths. He doesn't
speak English!"

The coolie heard this with a grin.

"Faith, me choild av sin!" he muttered to himself under his breath. "It's just loike a Japanese tu
say so. An' pwhat is it I shpake I'd loike to know?
P'rhaps you've mistuk it fur Oirish."

Hereupon he broke out into a plaintive Japanese
chaunt.

Tori mo kosanai
Genkai nada wo
Yarareru kono mi wa
Itowanedo :
Ato ni nokorishi
Tsuma ya ko wa
Dō shite tsuki-hi wo
Okuru yara.

All the while he kept a-crooning the catch he
was listening with all his ears.

"Whisht, ye divil!" he muttered to himself at
last, as he made another cast of the line. "It'll
froighten all the luvely little fishes, but it'll divert
suspicion."

Just then he looked round again. He had
noticed a huskiness in Ishida's voice and he was
aware that Furukawa's tongue had waxed thick in
his mouth, and that that gentleman had begun to
pay particular attention to the clearness of his arti-
culation, which is a pretty sure premonitory finger-
post on the way to being gloriously drunk.

"And so," hiccoughed Ishida, "we c-c-caught her. We r-r-ran her old uncle i-i-i-nto the pawn-shop and into d-d-d-ebt, till he had n-nothing and l-less to live upon and ———"

"And th-then?" queried his auditor.

"Th-then we s-sent them up to K-kiga to recu-cuperate, and then sh-she of course consented, and the w-wedding is to be on December 24th and I h-h-hope you'll c-c-come."

"Come! Of course I will!"

"An-and don't you th-think it was smart now,—*first-class* smart?"

The 'first-class' was fetched up from somewhere below the pit of the stomach with that harsh, grat-ing, scraping sound that the Japanese employ as an extra frill to the superlative degree.

"*Hontō ni* first-class smart!" rejoined Furukawa smacking his lips after another pull at the bottle.

The coolie's satisfaction was undoubted when Mr. F. rejected the glass as an intermediary and appealed to the fountain-head direct. He was advancing merrily and cheerily apace.

"Now then," (here he lifted the whiskey, nodded to Ishida san, put the bottle to his mouth, and turned it up till its bottom was on a level with the horizon at the top of the Fukara Pass.) "Now then, I'll t-t-tell you a better story than that. There was once upon a time a Japanese in foreign parts and he had a v-v-very good master, but he w-was a *baka*. And he——"

Here followed a long, disconnected, and tangled narrative in which Sunday-School, a shark, £27,000 and detectives played the leading parts. The narrator's voice waxed hoarse and husky towards the close. The coolie had turned bolt round, utterly forgetful of making a show of threshing the water.

Furukawa finished and Ishida snored applause. The story-teller looked at him pityingly.

"P-p-poor head!" he muttered. "But Ja-Japanese n-never will l-l-learn to drink!"

Then he too sunk forward in a limp and spineless heap. Mighty is the power of Garn-kirk Whiskey.

Just then the boat from Hakone was coming in about half-a-mile from the landing. The coolie looked at it and then at the two incapables on the beach. He went over to them and shook first one and then the other, and found them both inert and helpless alike.

"Now thin!" he proceeded to himself, as he not over-gently planted the toe of his sandal in the rear of Ishida's dwarfish anatomy. "If yez want me honest an' trutful opinion av yez, it's a mane little scutt yez are, tu play hankey-pankey thricks wid the good ould maan an' his purty niece as ye've just confessed

tu doin'. An' as fur you,"—(here he turned to
Furukawa, and punctuated his remarks with the toe
of his right foot) "it's sorry I am I cudn't allow
yez to get biled in yer iniquity loike a murphy in
its jacket. But policy's agin' it. No more can I lave
ye here in the cowld, fur ye moight die, and I'd
lose me sivin an twinty thousand pounds entoirely,
for I don't fancy ye've got it wid yez. I'll hev a
luk though!"

He bent down and went through Furukawa's
pockets like a footpad of a liberal education.

"As I thought," he said. "Only a few hundred
yen, and that's not good enough. But it's mesilf
that 'll fix yer honour in less than a week. Hoy!"
he shouted turning to the boat that was coming towards the landing some hundred yards from where
he stood. "Hoy! here's a cargo. It consists of
two *saké*-tubs."

The boat-men grinned, and came and carried
the incapables on board.

"Now thin!" said the coolie to himself with a
vicious tug at Mr. Furukawa's sprucely waxed
moustache. "Isn't it a foine rich crop av cat's
whishkers the vagabond's a-rearin'? An' faith, it's
all wid me own capital he's doin' it."

They rowed over to the Hotel in the village of
Hakone. The coolie got them ashore, both still
stertorously fuddled, and told the people that they

were gentlemen who had met with a slight accident. He charged the landlord to look after them carefully, saying he had business to attend to at Miyanoshita.

But as soon as he passed the gate of the courtyard of the inn he set his face towards the dip of the afternoon sun, which was right in the opposite direction. That evening he caught the train at Numadzu, and boarded it with a third class ticket for Kiōto.

VII.

Some ignorant and uninstructed scribblers have put it on record that there is no such thing as a marriage-ceremony in Japan. That this should be the case in a country where few men are bachelors, and no women are old maids, sounds passing strange. And in Japan many folks do not rest content with one single hit-or-miss shot at the white of the matrimonial target as all must do in Britain, many to their bitter woe. In Japan there is, on an average, one divorce for every three marriages;—behold, are not the figures of the *Résumé Statistique de l'Empire du Japon* at hand to lend verisimilitude to an otherwise bald and unconvincing statement?

It certainly would be odd if there were no marriage-ceremony in Japan, considering the tremendous amount of marrying and giving-in-marriage that goes on in the country. But there *is* such a thing as a marriage-ceremony, or rather there are several of them.

Some of the more aristocratic of these events stretch over nine days; that is, if we count in all the visits and return visits that have to be received and made.

But then it is not everybody that can afford to kill time in this fashion. Every one does not trouble about the ceremonies of the occasion, and hence the misguided and over-hasty generalization of the scribblers afore-mentioned. When the cook or the boy-san brings home a change of wife, for example, he doesn't waste any of his own or of his master's valuable hours in garnishing the event with any needless frilling. He is a busy individual, and man does not live and prosper by giving heed unto the *San-san-ku-do*, but by throwing himself with all the voracity of a pike upon squeezes, and perquisites, and upon opportunities of negotiating equitable treaties with the vegetable-hawker, the fishmonger, and the washerman.

But Ishida Taro, conscious of harbouring within himself the elements of greatness, and being a man minded to be correct and to observe the best usages of society as befitted one of its law-makers, thought well to furnish forth a feast, and to make his wedding a mile-stone on the social track of the year.

So his town-house in Koji-machi was made ready for the occasion, and Mr. Ishida assembled all his relations unto the third cousin removed, and all his friends and several of his enemies to witness his happiness and glory. For he wanted to make the hearts of those that hated him burn with malice and envy at beholding him pairing with such a mate as old Tanaka's niece, Ayame, was.

These two latter had returned from Hakone some short time before, and had been living in a small villa not far from Ishida's mansion. Here Ayame made her final preparations for the sacrifice.

The 24th of Dec. had been chosen for the 'lucky day,' after Mr. Ishida Shozo had secretly consulted the old soothsayer of Asakusa. For although Ishida san senior did not have any great faith in Chinese medicine as practised by himself, he had an un- bounded, albeit a sneaking confidence in fortune- telling and divination. And in this respect he was not by any means so very much out of touch with his generation as it might seem. Japanese, in com- mon with the rest of the world suffer much from the shades of their ancestors, steam-boats and railways, telegraphs and telephones, Parliaments, stove-pipe hats and the electric-light not-withstanding.

So on the afternoon of this 24th of December Ayame robed her all in white, as Japanese brides are wont to do. Of course white is the dress of mourning in Japan, which is just what might be expected according to the wide sweeping rule of contraries,—that unfailing guide to figuring out the true inwardness and general run of things in this country. This wedding-dress of white usually means that the bride dies to her own family, and that she will never leave her husband's house except as the protagonist in her own funeral.

But in Ayame's case it was a real and no figurative robing for the tomb. For her marriage with Ishida Taro, she told herself, meant death to her soul. When then, the maid servants began to wield the broom in sweeping out her uncle's house when Ishida Shozo and his wife came to bear her away at nightfall, she shudderingly said to herself that the ceremony was no mere make-believe. She was morally and intellectually doomed.

Ishida Shozo and his spouse took her in charge. In a quarter of an hour they reached the house where the marriage-feast was to be spread and where the marriage-guests were assembled to make merry. She was conducted within, and seated in the room where the ceremony was to be performed.

Soon the bridegroom expectant entered. He came into the chamber in all the glory of *embi-fuku* (swallow-tails) and white-necktie, and magnificent in his importance and pride. Then the marriage feast was served in all the orthodox courses from the clam soup, emblem of union, unto the last; and then came the *San-san-ku-do*, (three-times three, nine times). Ayame was pale, but wondrously calm withal as she raised the cups to her lips. In her sore trial she bore herself right bravely, as became a Samurai's daughter, and in keeping with the precepts of her uncle.

Then she retired to remove her own silken dress of white and to don a coloured one, the gift of her husband. Now the room where this had to be done had a window giving on the alley-way that ran between the house and the neighbouring one. The dress lay on a *kobuton* not far from the window. As she approached to take it up she saw a small square of paper lying on it. There was something written on it, in English too. She took it up and read it. What a thump her heart gave when she grasped its purport! It was short and in a few words, but it seemed to set her veins a-flow with fire. It ran :—

" *You are betrayed and cheated. Hirata is Ishida's banto. Ishida made him quarrel with your uncle. Ishida owns the Kinokuniya pawn-broker's shop, and* he stopped your uncle's credit in *Asakusa*. He is a fox, and it is all a trick. Do not marry Ishida Taro!"

As she looked at it, and read it and re-read it, the letters all seemed to run together in a blurred confusion of red. She felt as if she were going mad. She sat down for a moment to think. Just then an attendant entered to help her to dress. She rose mechanically and allowed herself to be clothed as if in a dream. Then she was marshalled into the room, almost unconscious of her actions and her surroundings, holding the astounding missive crumpled in her twitching fingers.

Once more she had to drink, or feign to drink. She took up the cup as if dazed. And then just as she raised it to her lips a wonder fell upon the throng.

The room was hushed into silence watching her intently, when upon the clear frosty air outside there broke a strain of weird and plaintive melody. Not a Japanese one; the words and tune were strange to most in the gathering. But Ayame knew it well.

As the beaker touched her lips she stopped, and with her great dark eyes all aglow with a living fire, she bent forward and listened with all her ears.

> "*Bonny Charlie's noo awa*
> *Safely ower the ragin' main*
> *Oh! my heart will break in twa*
> *Should he no come back again.*"

All this proceeded slowly, methodically, and with measured execution, till '*again*' faded away in a long-drawn wail.

All eyes were fixed on Ayame in amazement. The colour came back into her cheeks and her face broke into a smile joyous as the bursting of the Yezo meads into flowers in Spring. Then, as the last echoes died into nothingness, she dashed the cup from her, started to her feet, and with a thrilling cry of joy rushed from the room into the darkness of the outer night beyond.

"*As she gazed aloft, Ayame told herself that in yet two months he would be clothed in one great robe of shimmering white.*" (P. 185.)

They sought her baith by bower and ha';
The Ladie was' na seen!
She's ower the Border, and awa'
Wi' Jock o' Hazeldean.

PART III.

I.

It was an awkward *contretemps* for bridegroom and guests alike, but especially so beyond all telling for Ishida Shozo, the groom's father, who had acted as *nakōdo* or middleman in the business. Upon his shoulders the blame of this dire offence against the proprieties would fall with crushing weight. It would make him hide his head in shame for many and many a day. It was Ichabod with the glory of his renown as a match maker,—just too as he had achieved the crowning one of a long and masterly series of matrimonial diplomatic triumphs.

But guests and bridegroom and *nakōdo* and all were spared the *gêne* of doing nothing but looking at each other in silence, and finally all sidling out shamefacedly like the elders who brought the woman taken in adultery for judgment.

As Ayame rushed from the room her dress caught one of the large lamp-stands, and over the lamp went with a crash. The kerosene spread in a flood all over the mats, thoroughly soaking and saturating them. Then came an ominous ' *Wouf!* ' and the whole centre of the floor seemed to rise in a great bubble of sullen flame of the colour of blood in a dead ox's eye, and a smoke-burst shattered itself and filled the room with filth and stench and blindness. Then ensued a pandemonium of hoots and shouts, and the marriage guests emptied themselves in a tumbling cascade into the open. It was not a time to stand on ceremony or to study precedence. No one stood by bowing to the dust, and stretching out a deprecating hand, and murmuring ' *O saki!* ' (you honourably first!) It was a wild stampede, a rush for life, a save himself or herself who can, and fire take the hindmost. They burst and broke from the room with but one single thought, and that thought was safety.

All except one, that is. Mr. Furukawa had

started at the first note of the singing. He had watched Ayame closely as it proceeded, and so was not quite unprepared for her rush from the room. Who was the singer, and where had she gone?

These two questions followed each other like flashes in Furukawa's mind. He sprang up and dashed outside in quest of the answers.

But not a trace of Ayame was to be seen,—she had vanished as if into smoke, while in the street the only sound that broke the frosty stillness was the long-drawn, quavering notes of the blind shampooer's whistle, followed by his weird and wailing cry of '*Am-m-ma!*'

In his rush Furukawa came in contact with the caller, and,—how it was he could not understand— was astonished to find his own feet fly from under him and his head bump on the ground, and the stars in the vault of heaven to increase and multiply and wax in brilliance and variety of colour apace.

He lay stunned for an instant and then he gathered himself up and rushed back to the house. It was now a roaring crackling fire, lighting up the quarter with a ruddy glare, and sending a great snake-like column of smoke swirling aloft into the windless sky. Already the neighbouring fire-bell was clattering forth its insistent summons followed by one long, single stroke that seemed to vibrate and

quiver for minutes till the warning of its liquid notes
faded away in ripples.

And then again came the wild clash and clang
and clatter, still more insistent than before. And
now all the bells in the neighbouring wards have
found their tongues and the rabbit hutches below
them begin to look like hives in swarming-time.
With a roar and a rush and a jangle of bells and
harness, the fire-engine comes rumbling on the scene,
and opens on the blazing rafters, for even in this
short time the fire had got so far.

However the contest was short though sharp.
The night was deadly still without a breath of wind,
and the flames shot up straight and fair. Hence
the danger to the neighbourhood was slight. The
fire began and ended with Ishida's villa, but it made
a pretty thorough-going job of that.

❈   ❈   ❈   ❈

When Furukawa rushed back from his futile
chase he met with an odd reception from his friend
Ishida Taro. Furukawa had gone up to him with
words of sympathy on his tongue. But Ishida
turned upon him like a wild cat in an evil temper.

"Sh!" whispered Furukawa warningly. "Be
quiet. The guests are all watching you, and the
crowd besides. Don't lose your composure and
become undignified."

"Undignified!" literally screamed Ishida, evidently out of his wits with passion. "This is a fine piece of work! Ah! you cheat, you traitor, and you trickster!"

Ishida jumped about as he said this, his left hand excitedly waving his tall chimney-pot hat which he had contrived to rescue in the rush.

Furukawa's eye gleamed with an ugly light at this sally. He stepped forward and laying a powerful and restraining hand upon the other's arm asked him what he meant by these terms.

"Mean? Mean, do you ask? What the words always mean. You see you're found out! Look at that!"

With a wrench he shook himself free from Furukawa's fingers, and spreading out a twist of paper he was holding in his clenched right fist, he held it up with both hands before the other's face. In his excitement he dropped his hat and it rolled into the gutter behind him.

Furukawa read the writing with amazement writ large in every line of his face. It was the note Ayame had found when she retired to change her dress. She had dropped it together with the cup when she dashed that and its contents on the floor.

"You needn't act!" panted Ishida. "You're found out! You're—"

"Stop!" shouted Furukawa. "What *do* you mean, man?"

"You're a beast of a traitor! Isn't that your hand-writing? Can you deny it? See here, look at this!"

He pulled out a letter Furukawa had written him a few days before and placed it alongside the mysterious missive. There was something more than even a strong family resemblance between the two pieces of caligraphy.

Furukawa started in spite of himself.

"Yes!" Ishida screamed. "You're the cause of all this. "You————.""

"I assure you," said Furukawa, "on my word of honour, I know nothing about it at all. Let us go and talk it over quietly. Some————.""

"Talk it over quietly! Know nothing of it! Oh! you can act, you liar! But you did it. It's your handwriting. Besides who knew but you? You liar and traitor!"

Under the circumstances it is possible that Mr. Furukawa might have been inclined to make some little allowances for his friend's sorry plight, notwithstanding the slightly objectionable cast of the phraseology he expressed himself in. But unfortunately Ishida Taro though fit to emphasize it and punctuate it with Exclamation-marks in the shape of three blows directed at Furukawa's head.

Now when it comes to settling a difference of opinion in this fashion, the home-bred Japanese is at a hopeless disadvantage. In days of old, when every samurai had a pair of swords, and when no sword ever left its sheath unless strictly on business, it was different. In adjusting a tiff such as the present, the old time Japanese, according to all accounts, was at once deft, workmanlike, and expeditious. But in a street-row conducted on approved modern scientific principles the Japanese has yet a lot to learn. From a British stand-point he is simply not in it. It is not that he lacks pluck ; it is simply because he does not know how. He will clutch and claw, and jump and peck like a bantam,—and possibly once on a time vary the slap of the open hand with a blow of the clenched fist. But he will unfailingly make the cardinal mistake of letting his hand get above his head or away behind his shoulder to lend force to the argument. And that was just what, with all the best intentions in the world, Ishida Taro did.

Now Mr. Furukawa had been abroad in Anglo-Saxon countries where boxing is reckoned among the fundamentals of a liberal education, and in this particular respect Furukawa had acquired no mean measure of the learning of the Egyptians. Wherefore when his friend waxed over-emphatic and embarrasing in the expression of his sentiments,

Mr. F. just hauled off one step, and let his left come
out like the piston-rod of a steam engine. It
caught Ishida on the jaw, and he tumbled backwards
on the ruins of his tile in the gutter, feeling as if a
Hokkaido pony had got home on his face with a
hind-hoof. He lay there like a log of wood. It
was a cold and cheerless bed for a man on his
wedding-night.

Then Furukawa turned away. The other marriage guests gradually dispersed. It was a lively
function they had assisted at, but notwithstanding
they felt aggrieved. For the programme had not
been carried out strictly in accordance with the
original play-bill.

II.

When you emerge from the Shimbashi Railway Terminus, you turn to the left, and then to the right, and passing over a bridge not without reminiscences of the 'straight and narrow path,' you find yourself in Ginza, the chief, and if the truth be told, the only modern street in the metropolis of Japan. In Europe it would be entered in the category of the 'poor but respectable,' but Japan is immensely proud of it. However that is not the point at present.

But if the globe-trotter can make up his mind to forego the rococo splendours of Ginza, and immediately on passing the bridge above-mentioned turn to the left along the canal, he will see something that is really Japanese. Furthermore something worth looking at, that is supposing the honourable bird of passage strikes the place at the right hour of the day—or of the night—and has besides the further additional insignificant qualification of possessing eyes to see. For upon this canal debouch the half-dozen lanes that, with their alley-ways and labyrinths, make up the far-famed Shimbashi *geisha* quarters.

These consist of some hundred and thirty 'houses,' or establishments. They are all pretty much of the same style of architecture, small, two-storied erections, big enough for sizeable doll's-houses. In front of each of them hangs a great globe-like paper lantern, often with curious metal-work on its top and bottom, and liberally be-powdered with a sprinkling of Chinese characters and Japanese *hiragana*, or cursive script. This is the sign-board of the establishment. Many of these carry names that boast of an antiquity far exceeding that of two-thirds of the parvenu titles of the five or six hundred gentlemen who enjoy the privilege of legislating by hereditary right for some forty millions of 'free-born' British subjects. For however much in other respects Japan may change her institutions, the names of her famous *geisha* houses remain fixed and stablished.

Above the door and under the eaves of the house are ranged the wooden 'name-cards' of the inmates. Where the eye can peep through a half-opened lattice, it lights upon flower-vases here and there, a stray *shamisen* perhaps, and as often as not a whole church-full of tinsel Buddhistic religious furniture in one of the alcoves. For it must be recorded that whatever their shortcomings in other things, in their devotions and in their orisons these ladies are highly exemplary.

Besides, right in the centre of the quarter is a quaint little temple to *Inari-sama*, the Fox-god.

But it is the bath-house standing next door to it that plays the all-important part in the social economy of the community.

O-Kiku-san had just returned from this *yudono* (bath-house), where she had heard all the gossip of the day. For in Japan, in the matter of news-mongering, the bath-house takes the place held by the barber's shop in Athens of old, and by the black-smith's and the tavern in an English village. There O-Kiku-san had been felicitated with many honor-

ifics and no small amount of heart-burning on her
latest conquest, of which the newspapers were full.
The *Yomiuri Shimbun* devoted several six-inch
columns of chops to setting forth the romance,
while in the *Yamato*, the episode attracted far
more attention than its attack on the Government
which earned for it an unexpected and unprofitable
three weeks' holiday.

It was only Kotake-san that had proved unbear-
ably nasty. But then, no doubt, she had her ex-
cuses for being jealous. She had greeted O-Kiku-
san with an abnormally low obeisance and in the
most honied of accents had expressed a hope ;—

"That as to her (Kotake) unworthy old pair of
geta, she (O-Kiku-san) did not experience any inconvenience from wearing them."

So O-Kiku-san had returned to her quarters
with anger and mortification. Her feelings were
not inconsiderably ruffled. As she proceeded to
lay on the *beni* (pigment) on her lips as she knelt
before the mirror after her maid had painted her
neck a snowy white with the regulation three brown
Vandyke-collar points at the vertex of the spine,
the long-drawn wail of the shampooer's whistle
sounded forth from the darkness. Then came the
'tap, tap, tap,' of the staff on the ground, and the
weird and melancholy call of '*Am-m-ma!*' O-Kiku-
san paused for a moment, and then slid a *shoji* open
and looked into the street. She then turned to her
maid and told her :—

"That calling the *Amma-san* would be good!"

The girl took the hint, and in a minute, the 'tap,
tap, tap,' the shuffling of feet in the *genka*, and the
sound of hands feeling the walls announced the
entrance of the worthy functionary.

He opened the *shoji*, and kneeling down made
his obeisance. O-Kiku-san looked at him with
approval. Barring his blindness, he was a fine specimen of a man, with broad chest, square shoulders,
arms sinewy and much longer than Japanese arms
are wont to be. Even his face was not uncomely,

for the shades he wore over his sightless eyes concealed the glassy stare that makes looking upon
blindness a pain. He thought fit to explain and
apologise for this peculiarity.

"Because it is windy to-night and because the dust
is inconvenient to my unworthy eyes, I have put on
this shade. Pray excuse my rudeness in so doing."

O-kiku-san answered '*Do Itashimashite! Waka-
rimashita;*' and after sending her maid out for
the evening, lay down at full length on the
mats and submitted herself unto the shampooer's
fingers. He sidled over beside her, threw back
his sleeves, and began to finger and rub, and

knead and prod, exploring all the geography of her well-fashioned anatomy. She took up the *Yomiuri*, and gave herself up to the joy of fame as dispensed by the newspaper reporter and his first assistant, the Printer's Devil, both artists in hieroglyphics.

In a short time the *Amma san* and the *Yomiuri* utterly effaced all recollection of Kotake and her vicious pin-pricks. Just as the shampooer's task drew to a close, the wicket of the door-way was thrown open with a whirr, and shot back again from the inside. Then followed the shuffling noise of stepping off from first one *geta* and next from the other, and then the *shoji* was thrust aside, and O-kiku's new *danna-san* (master), Furukawa, strode into the room.

The *geisha* sat up and bowed, and then saying that she was going into the adjoining room to dress, suggested that Furukawa san should 'honourably receive a shampooing.' The *Amman san* seconded the proposal with a flood of beseeching honorifics, and the new arrival gave a grumpy assent, and threw himself down on the floor in a position to further operations.

The *Amma san* set to work tapping and kneading.

"Now, then!" growled the patient, who was evidently not in the most even of tempers. "Can't you do your work in a rational and civilized fashion?

Why don't you shampoo *up* instead of shampooing *down?* Don't you know that one aim of real scientific work of this sort is to bring the blood lingering in the superficial veins back to the centre? But you stay-at-home uneducated Japanese *will* persist in making the country ridiculous in spite of all we who travel to study foreign civilization can do to prevent it. You are simply a set of old played-out conservative semi-barbarians!"

When in an ill humour, Furukawa gave way unto the weakness of parading his superiority. He would then flout his untravelled countrymen without let or stay, and as often as not without rhyme or reason. But in this particular case he was right,— that is, as far as his text went. But the commentary and the general remarks he garnished it with, were wrong-headed and misguided to a degree.

The Amma san bowed, sucked in his breath and said *"Gomen-nasai! Domo! Osore-irimashita!* What clever men you great travellers are!"

Then he went on, beating and prodding and rubbing as directed. He worked up towards his patient's neck, cautiously and with care. Then as he reached it, his right-hand fingers suddenly clutched Furukawa's wind-pipe and squeezed it tight, while with his left, the shampooer caught him by the hair of the head, and bumped his face on the mats with the force of a baby steam-hammer.

He kept his grip on the throat, till Furukawa was purple in the face. Then when he gave no further sign of life, the *Amma san* got up, and producing a coil of string of a strand nearly akin to a rope, tied his hands behind his back and generally trussed him up as is the wont of Japanese policemen to deal with their captives. Then he turned him over on his back, and reseating himself on his hams, brought out his pipe and tobacco-pouch and began to roll a pill for the bowl.

He knocked out several fills, watching Furukawa all the time.

" Musha, it's mesilf that hopes I haven't sent him tu kingdom come and glory for ever!" he muttered to himself uneasily, as Furukawa continued to lie as still a log.

At last Furukawa heaved a heavy sigh and opened his eyes. He made an effort to sit up and look about him, but without success. The shampooer reached forward, took him by the breast of his dress, and pulled him into a squatting posture.

Furukawa looked at the *Amma-san* with dazed wonderment. The patches were gone from his face and a pair of twinkling eyes seemed to pierce him through like gimlets. He winked with his own eyelids to make sure that he was waking. It seemed more like a bad nightmare than anything else.

He looked steadily at the shampooer for half-a-minute, evidently taking in his every line and feature.

" Kichibei!" at last he stammered with a gasp.

" Yes, that's me!" answered the coolie quietly in English.

Furukawa threw up his head in quick astonishment.

" But I thought you knew no English except 'D—n it all'"? he went on in the tone of a question.

" Ah! but that was more than a fortnight ago; an' I have been takin' lessons since then. Don't you know that there are Japanese tachers who tache you the whole language in twinty lessons?"

The coolie's eyes danced with mischief as he said this.

Furukawa paused in fresh astonishment.

" Now, will you be good enough to explain all this nonsense?" he said at last.

" This *pœhat*, did yez say? This how much?"

There was a ring of ironical menace in the words that was not pleasant.

" Will you be good enough to explain all this nonsense?" repeated the other raising his voice, and uttering his request in a tone of angry command.

" Can't!" curtly returned Kichibei, with a vicious 'pan!' 'pan!' on the *hibachi*.

" Why not?"

"'Cause it isn't nonsense, at all, at all, as you'll soon percave, Mr. Takahashi!"

Furukawa's face became sallow. He shifted about as if his position were hurting him.

"Mr. Takahashi! My name is not Takahashi. It is Furukawa."

"May be it is. Japanese are rather given to changing their names, aren't they,—especially about conscription toime? But you were Takahashi until that shark swallowed yez in Sydney harbour wid me own sivin an' twinty thousand thousand-pound notes in yer pocket."

Furukawa could scarcely refrain from crying out.

"Who are you then?" he asked.

"Kichibei av the Naraya, av coorse. But if yez really want tu know who I am whin I'm at home, it's O'Rafferty they call me,—Mr. Phelan O'Rafferty, —Phelan O'Rafferty Esq., owner av the *Komachi*, and late av the Broken Hill Silver Moine. An' I'll throuble yez fur me sivin and twinty thousand-pounds, wid interest at tin per cent up tu date!"

While he was talking, Furukawa had pulled himself together pluckily.

"Well, Mr. Phelan O'Rafferty," he remarked quietly, "you're evidently a very ingenious individual, but you've made a mistake. I don't know anything about Sydney, I never heard of you before, and as for your 'sivin an twinty thousand pounds' (here Furukawa mimicked him to a miracle), 'faith! an' it's mesilf that belaves they're the product av a disased imagination."

O'Rafferty, for answer, edged round and threw back a sleeve of his *yukata* that had hitherto concealed his sash. The handle of a six-shooter came into view.

"Faith, thin, me son," he remarked coolly enough, "this gun av mine is given to goin' off accidental-loike whin folks spake av it's owner dispoitefuily. An' the chances are ye'll find yersilf in the loine av its fire whin it takes it into its head tu begin the afore-mentioned performance. Div yez moind me now?"

"What if I call the police and hand you over to them for attempted robbery?"

"What if I call the police and hand *you* over to them for *actual* robbery to the tune av sivin an' twinty thousand pounds, me son?"

Furukawa laughed scornfully.

"I would advise you not to do any such thing. In the first place I know nothing of the cock-and-bull story trumped up by your diseased imagination, and in the next, supposing for a moment it were true, which it isn't, there's no extradition between Japan and Australia!"

"Exthradition be blowed!" broke out O'Rafferty with a contemptiuous wave of his arm. "Exthradition! As if Phelan O'Rafferty made any account av lawyer's thruck av that description! But yez won't be reasonable and own-up?"

Furukawa's only answer was a satirical laugh.

"All right, me son! Thin, if yez really and truly wish tu give work tu the hangman, it's not mesilf that 'ull stand in the way av yer executin' yer laudable project."

He clapped his hands and sat waiting. Furukawa gave an uneasy sidle on the mats. A moment afterwards his face became almost livid when the *shoji* were thrust open in response to O'Rafferty's summons.

III.

"Come in, and sit here, please!" said the Irish-man to the girl who appeared.

She was evidently a *geisha*, possibly about twenty or twenty-one years of age.

"Now, me frind!" he went on turning to Furu-kawa. "Let me presint an ould acquaintance av yours. This is O-Matsu-san av the Massudaya from Kioto. I think ye've seen her before; the last time in 1886, if I'm not misinformed."

It was astonishing to see the change that came over Furukawa while this presentation was being made. All his flippant jauntiness evanesced, and

he collapsed like a full-blown bladder pricked by a
pin. O'Rafferty smiled a smile of derisive mirth,
while his eyes twinkled with mischief more lumi-
nously than before.

"You know this young lady, don't yez Mr. Takahashi?" he asked meaningly.

"No! I don't. I have not that honour," he replied huskily.

"No!" said O'Rafferty. "I thought ye'd lie
about the mather. It's a bashful young maan yez
are."

Then he turned to the *geisha*.

"Have you ever met this beautiful young gentleman before?"

The girl was looking at Furukawa closely. At last
she slowly shook her head, and said hesitatingly;—

"I don't think so. He is not unlike Akadani who
killed my sister, but I don't think it is the same."

"Hey!" said O'Rafferty evidently much put
out. "What do you say?"

Furukawa's face had lighted up like a landscape
when the sun comes out from behind a rain-cloud
in spring.

"Please show me that photograph!" said O'Rafferty stretching out his hand.

The *geisha* fumbled in the folds of her *obi*
and brought forth a pocket-book. Its contents
were varied in kind and many in number. There

were cosmetics, a little-looking glass, some stray hair-pins, scents, a medicine-box, and a bundle of photographs,—some of them, if the truth be told, not over-decent in character. These latter she took out, and placing the pocket-book in her lap, she ran through the series like one manipulating a pack of cards.

"There!" she said at last, stopping and handing a *carte de visite* to O'Rafferty.

The Irishman directed alternate glances at it and at Mr. Furukawa, who sat looking at him with an ugly and unpleasing scowl.

"So!" at last broke out O'Rafferty. "I see how it is! Here he is in true *yakusha* rig, wid plain face, shaven oiye-brows, and ould toime cue on the top av him. But four years and a crop av cat's whiskers raised on me own capital have worked changes."

Then he again turned to the girl with a bow.

"Will you have the goodness to retire for ten minutes and come again when I call you?" he said.

The girl replied '*Shōchi itashimashita,*' and withdrew.

"Now, thin, me frind," began the Irishman addressing himself to Furukawa, "I'll throuble yez to submit to an operation. I thought it moight be necessary in the coorse av the drama, an' so I came wid the requisite tools."

He plunged into one of the recesses of his garments and therefrom he brought forth a razor, a shaving-brush and a cake of soap.

"What are you going to do?" Furukawa asked with much apprehension in his tone.

"Do? Why, shave yez, av coorse! Do yez think I can't? Are yez afraid av an accident? There may be wan, if ye're skittish, but if ye're quiet an' orderly, it's the poethry av motion depicted on yer chin I'll show yez. As a barber I boast mesilf tu be no new chum, fur it's many av me frinds the Tommies I've scraped, whin the rig'mintal shaver was down wid D. T.'s which was a throuble he occasionally suffered systematically from. Besoides it's New Year's toime, an' all the Tokyo barbers are busy and couldn't or wouldn't come, even tho' I axed them in court language itsilf. An' besoides they'd mistake yez fur a Furriner, an' charge yez treble prices, which 'ud be mortal hard on a pore man, which ye'll undoubtedly be to-morrow mornin' at this toime."

While thus running on, O'Rafferty was vigorously licking up a lather.

"Arrah now! Be aisy!" he said as Furukawa ducked to one side when he approached to lay it on. "The razor's sharp an' maybe ye'll get cut an' wounded."

"Now thin!" he broke forth angrily as his

victim paid scant heed to his warning. "Now thin! I'll tell yez pwhat!" (Here he laid down the brush, and putting his hands on his knees glared fiercely into the other's eyes.) "If yez don't hould steady, I'll take yez by the troat, an' I'll hould it till ye're as still as a glorified mummy and *thin* I'll undress yer ugly mug fur yez! Div yez moind me now?"

The remonstrance was not without its effect. Furukawa became submissive and dumb like a sheep before his shearer, and in a trice his 'cat's whiskers,' and eke his waxed moustache and all the glory of his beard had passed from him.

"Now, thin!" went on O'Rafferty whetting the razor and gazing admiringly at his handiwork. "Whoever sez it isn't a first-class job, 'ull have to foight me, Phelan O'Rafferty Esq., owner av the *Komachi*, an' artist in hair. Next for the oiye-brows and the scalp-lock."

He fetched off the hair above the eyes, ploughed a furrow along the top of the head, and then setting to work with the "ile" as he called it, he brought a real old-time top-knot into being. Then he appealed to the photograph.

"Yes!" he chuckled. "It 'ull do! It 'ull do! Hoy! O-Matsu-san!"

The girl entered once more. As soon as her eyes lighted on Furukawa she gave a cry.

"Akadani! Akadani, of the Nakamuraza, the man that killed my sister!"

IV.

"*So desu ka?*" said O'Rafferty with a rising into-
nation that indicated triumph achieved after difficulties surmounted. "Well now, me dear! you'll
just go outside, and wait and do as I've tould yez."

When she had gone, he turned to Furukawa with
a laugh.

"Now, me son! What do you say tu callin' the
pōlice *now*? Who's top-sawyer at prisint, I'd loike
tu ask yez. Do yez own up?"

Furukawa signified with a groan that he did.

"Exthradition!" went on O'Rafferty flipping his
fingers contemptuously. "Exthradition an' such-

like pettifoggin' lawyer's tricks fur Phelan O'Rafferty! Not much!"

"Now I'll tell yez," he went on sinking his voice
to a confidential tone. "It's a mather av 12,000
yen av me sivin-an'-twinty thousand pounds ye've
spint, not reckonin' interest. Ye've got just a
hundred and sixty-one thousand *yen* to yer credit
at the Nihon Ginko. The cashier there's a frind
av mine; so I know, and yez needn't be so bashful
as tu deny it. Well, I've had lots av fun chasin'
yez,—far more than in rabbit-shootin', or in bear-
huntin' or in any such-like similar thruck, always
savin' and exceptin' boat-sailin', fur that takes the
cake widout any doubt. Do yez admit that?"

O'Rafferty glowered at him sternly, ready to
meet and grapple with contradiction. But Furukawa was wise.

"Of course, I do!" he said "What intelligent
man *could* doubt it?"

"Now, thin," exclaimed O'Rafferty his grim
looks breaking up into a smile of boyish pleasure.
"Thim's the wurruds av a maan av sinse! It's
worth just a thousand dollars to yez, that remark
is. Pwhat I was purceedin' tu say was this:—
Ye've given me sport,—moighty foine sport, and
whoever sez Phelan O'Rafferty does not stand up
and pay fur his sport loike a maan, lies in his troat.
Now," he went on producing a cheque-book, "here

I've drawn a cheque payable tu mesilf for a hundred and sixty thousand, an' it's all complete barrin' the thriflin' mather av your signature. Av coorse, yersilf's not the maan tu mar and dishturb the harmony av the sayson by widhouldin' it, are yez?"

O'Rafferty's appeal was at once wheedling, caressing, and persuasive. Furukawa felt it to be irresistible and graciously intimated as much.

"Now, thin," went on the Irishman carefully putting the document away in one of the recesses of his pot-bellied pocket-book, "it's yersilf that's the jewel av a maan tu get on wid! You see I intended tu leave you a thousand *yen* fur yersilf, but as ye're a sinsible maan in the mather av boats I'll make it two. I'll give you the extra thou, if yez meet me when the Bank opens to-morrow. But thin, after that, take note! It's now the winter sayson, an' all the boats are laid up, an' there'll be no more fun till May. There's no interprise in this counthry. Well, that bein' so, I've nothin' tu do but to pot at quail and wild-duck and pheasant, an' that's to me much loike what bein' kissed by a maan widout a moustache is tu a gurl. It's not satisfyin' at all, at all. An' I *must* have sport. Now I'll tell yez:— I don't care tin cints fur the outraged majesty av the law, an' I don't care a sixpince though ye'd played Jack the Ripper wid all the *geisha* in Kiyoto. If ye'd slaughter thim all, it 'ud be good fur the morals av the counthry at large. But as I've remarked before, I loike sport, and next tu boat-sailin' man-huntin's the foinest thing I've tuk a hand in. So I want more av it. Now, it's just three days start I'll give yez, and thin I'm afther yez fur murder agin. Sivinty-two hours from the minute I hand yez that other thousand dollars at the Bank tu-morrow,—thim's me own very wurruds! Look out and the Lord preserve yez, me son! Div yez moind me now?"

Furukawa nodded comprehension.

"But what about detectives or policemen?" he asked.

"About *pwhat?*" angrily shouted O'Rafferty starting up from his seat. "Div yez take me fur a lump av unadulterated maneness? Div yez think I'd encourage poachers an' scum av that sort? Did I have recoorse tu detectives an' sich tu get back me money which they all thought was sailin' about in the hould av a shark's belly? Man, if it were a fair match, I'd foight yez fur insultin' me by such a suggistion."

O'Rafferty again seated himself, and sat glowering over at Furukawa, the fingers of his two hands interlaced and one thumb twiddling round the other all the while.

"You are a wonderful man!" the actor ventured

at last, after he had watched O'Rafferty's silence for a minute or two.

"Faith, an' it's yersilf that knows how tu tickle wan in the right place!" responded the Irishman quickly, evidently highly pleased with the compliment.

"How did you ever get upon my track? But perhaps that's a delicate question."

"Not at all, me son! But it's a long story an' talkin's dhry work. Let's have a dhrink an' I'll sketch yez the outlines."

O'Rafferty clapped his hands and ordered the best *saké* in the house. Then he filled up a tumbler for Furukawa, and after performing a similar kindly office for himself, he proceeded.

"I've got a frind called Gifford. I'm good enough fur tactics, but he's the bhoy fur the strathegy. When it comes tu thinkin' out a thing I'm nowhere beside him."

"He must have a head!" put in Furukawa admiringly.

"He has!" replied O'Rafferty emphatically. "It's as big as a prize-turnip or the hat av a stone-lantern. Well, he planned fur me an' I carried out. He found yez were doin' the Daimio av Fusi-yama in 'Frisco and I wint there. Thin ye wint tu New Orleans, and thin New York an' thin mostly everywhere an' I was at yer heels purty closely.

I'd got ready tu dhrop on yez loike a sack av pota-
toes, or a mountain avalanche whin ye gave me
the slip an' cleared. What was that fur, I'd loike
tu know? Did yez know I was huntin' yez?"

"No, I didn't!" answered Furukawa ruefully.
"If I had, you'd never have caught me."

"Are yez quite sure av that now?" asked
O'Rafferty evidently nettled and ruffled at what he
held to be an under-estimate of his powers. "But
why then did yez up-tail and run?"

"I found out that a Sydney Detective was in
'Frisco, and was told that he was watching me."

"An' so, bein' accustomed tu wummen's parts
from av ould, ye bought shtays an' petticoats an'
a wig, and shipped as a lady-passenger on the
Tartaric!"

Furukawa started with wonder.

"How do you know that?"

"All along of a bit av an accident. Young ladies
should never meddle wid poets or parsons, an'
never wid them two combined in wan person. You
helped me out wid the tail av a pome, an' your
purty hand-writin' gave you away."

"And you were the Rev. Paul Julius?"

"The same at yer service, me young lady!"

"Well, I'll be hanged!"

"You will, most loikely, when I catch yez next
toime."

" Then how did you run across me after that ?"

" By persiverance, an' the help av Kotake! "

" Kotake! "

" Yes, av course. I knew your own spicial wake-ness, and so I wint as a *hakoya* (box-carrier). Thin whin you had your slight difference wid Kotake she tould me about yez. 'Twould seem ye're givin' tu shpakin' in yer slape. It's a baad habit whin ye've secrets on yer sowl. Thin I wint up to Miyano-shita, an' if't hadn't been fur me your bones 'ud be soup at this moment."

O'Rafferty paused to fill the old pipe he pro-duced from one of the recesses of his tatterdemalion robes. Furukawa said nothing; he could only gaze at him with rising wonder.

" Well, thin I heard yez tell Ishida—that's a mane little vagabone, much worse than you, 'cause ye're redeemed by a manly taste fur yachtin'—I heard yez tell him that ye were to take on wid that gurl O-Kiku-san. Well, I gave her two hundred *yen* to thrap yez, which she's done beautifully. Oh! no! you won't kill *her ;* it wouldn't pay. It 'ud be tu aisy to catch yez, 'cause the police are no sports an' never give a man any handicap at all, at all,—unless they can't help it. An' I don't want to have thim lubbers interferin' wid me own divarsion. Hullo! though, pwhat was that ? "

Just then there was a rapid movement in the

other room.　O'Rafferty jumped up, and dashed
to the door.

V.

" Begorrah!" he said, returning, " there's been an eaves-dhropper. It's that little scutt Ishida too. You stay here till I come back; I mane tu thrack him fur he's up to mischief beloike."

He dashed out and Furukawa was left alone.

To him it seemed as if he had just escaped from an earthquake of first-rate magnitude, that had merely had the grace to spare his life in the general havoc it made of his fortunes. For O'Rafferty had smitten and spared not,—or at least only to the extent of a beggarly two thousand dollars.

In a quarter of an hour the Irishman returned,

He was excited, waving his arms like a semaphore trying to be eloquent.

"Now, luk here! The programme's all changed! That little bla'guard has gone to the office an' tould the police what he's dhropped on by playin' the shpy wid his ears av a mule. So you'll have tu up an' cut. An' as there's just as much fun in foolin' the foorce as in huntin' you, I think you'll have me wid you, instead av agin you. Av course you and Ishida have quarrelled an' miscalled each other till the limited resources av Japanese swearwords were exhausted!"

"How do you know that?"

"Only I guessed it! Didn't he accuse you of shplittin' on him tu the gurl about Hirata and the pawn-shop?"

"Yes, but how do you know?"

"Och! Shure, I heard him tell yez in confidence when you got blind dhrunk the both av yez at Hakone. So I just dhropped the gurl a loine or two, an' I made it as loike your hand as I cud; for I'm a bit av an artist mesilf, an' I've spint a dale av toime in the study av your caligraphy."

"The Devil!" muttered Furukawa. "Great is Phelan O'Rafferty!"

For Furukawa was a sharp man, and quick and deft at sizing up character, and O'Rafferty was a deal more than a little vain. Wherefore the actor thought that compliments would pay, and he was right. Inwardly he was cursing himself for a thick-thumbed bungler all the while, and longing, oh! so ardently, to get even. And he meant to too, though it might cost him a lot.

"Yes, that was a nate job, though I sez it mesilf as shouldn't! It 'ud have lifted the roof av Silver's Theayter in Dublin itsilf! An' wasn't me execution av the song foine too?"

"Execution of the song? Were *you* there?"

"Av course! Didn't yez fall over a pore ould *amma-san* (blind shampooer) and get hurt? That was me. But ye'd better be changin' yer clothes, fur if we gabble much longer the policemen 'ull be here to call on yez. Tumble into them as fast as yez can, while I go on tellin' yez the plan av campaign."

The actor took the hint and began to metamorphose himself with the skill and agility that come only to a professional.

"Now, thin!" proceeded O'Rafferty. "Ye'll catch the train fur Yokohama, at wanst. Get out at Tsurumi,—there's no pōlice there—and walk on to Kanagawa and get on board the *Komachi*. There's poipes, an' baccy, an' beer, an' books, an' everything, an' there's the key av the lockers. They'll never luk fur yez there, an' to-morrow I'll come down with the funds fur the thrip you're tu take, to South

Ameriky, let us say.　Now be off wid you, an' the Lord bless you, though it's little I ever thought I'd be sayin' that tu the thafe that shtole me dividends!"

When the two policemen came half-an-hour later they found the house dark and silent. They entered and searched, and searched, but never an Akadani was to be found in it. For Mr. Akadani was at that time lying in O'Rafferty's own bunk on board the *Komachi*, eloquently but impotently cursing her owner.

Gifford had suddenly risen to fame. When he reached head-quarters in New York he had been lectured about over-staying his time in Japan. Now, Gifford hated nothing worse than a lecture, save perhaps good advice or sermons. Wherefore he waxed angry. And when the head of the Company went on in his foolhardiness to throw out a dark hint about 'closing engagements' if such a thing happened again, the artist rose to the full stretch of his 5 ft. 11 in. and coolly told him to look upon that operation as just that moment summarily performed. For it was not Gifford's way to take sauce from any one, saving O'Rafferty,—and perhaps a stray woman or two. He lit a cigar, drew on his gloves, and sauntered out of the office with the appearance of a man provokingly at peace with himself and all the world.

"Well, little lady!" he muttered to himself as he tossed away the stump of his weed, after taking the dimensions of the situation. "It's five thousand gold dollars a year with exs. that that picture of yours is going to cost me. I misdoubt me much if it was really worth that figure though. But the beggar checked me, and that's just what my own mother's son can't abear even for a little bit."

He paused for a moment in his walk to light a second Havana. Then as he paced onward he resumed.

"Now, I fancy I'll just go on to the village over the water and see what's to be done there. I wonder if I could fetch John Bull with an Exhibition."

That night he went on the *Umbria*. In less than a month, he found himself a good many rungs up the ladder of success.

He opened an exhibition in Bond Street and John Bull and his wife flocked thither to see and to buy. He made friends with our 'art critic,' and got praised in the newspapers. He was invited out, and he went into society. And when at the end of a short three months he found himself with not an unsold water-colour on his hands, and a balance of over £2,000 in his favour at the London and Westminster, he began to bless Japan, for Japan had been good unto him. He made up his mind to return, for like must men, although he had raved and railed at the country while a sojourner therein, his soul yet hungered and thirsted for it,—aye, even in spite of its *daikon*, its raw fish, its smells, and its 'more ten cents' way of doing business.

But there was a still more potent loadstone tugging him Eastward. He did not tell people that the finest piece of his work in Japan had not been put on exhibition at all. He knew that during the last week he had spent at Misaki he had done that which was far beyond any previous effort of his,— what was as likely as not to prove the high-water mark of the cunning of his brush for years to come, perhaps for ever. But he could not bring himself to expose that to the view of all the world and his wife. Although he was convinced that that study of Ayame would add whole cubits to his artistic stature, yet he stubbornly refrained from growing and waxing great at the price. The truth was that all of a sudden he had become over-qualmish; a few months before he would have laughed at any such scruples as the silliest sentimental moonshine. Then to him everything was simply so much raw material for his talent; so much flesh and blood, and colour and pose that had to be treated merely from the point of 'art for art's sake.' But from the day that this Japanese girl who talked teleology like a Hypatia, and who took to Homer as a duckling to water, had all for the mere love of *his* art, made a sacrifice that women of her class would ordinarily never dream of making, and made it too with such unalloyed sweetness and simplicity, it had begun to break on Gifford that there was something behind it all, greater and purer and mightier than his hitherto triumphant shibboleth of 'art for art's sake.'

So that study of Ayame was to him even as a sacred thing. Since it had been put on board the *Komachi*, no eyes had profaned it; not even O'Rafferty's. When no one was near he would often lock himself into the small 'den' off the studio he had rented, and gaze upon it for half-hours at a stretch. And then when he went to sleep it would fill his dreams with visions of that gentle face, so lovely in its simplicity and single-minded purity.

So when early one December evening the *Ancona* passed Oshima, Gifford stood watching the flashes from Jogashima. The wind was whistling down the Tōkiō Wan, its breath icy cold. How one's face smarted under its stinging lash as it shrilled and screamed aloft among the shrouds! But all unheed-

ing, Gifford's solitary great-coat kept the deck till
Tsurugi-saki dropped astern. Then he went below,
with his heart singing a wordless song of glee.

Next morning he landed. He found that fame
had run before him. The morning journal had a
friendly and flattering notice of his arrival, while
he was told that the reporter of the Evening
News wished to interview him. Gifford submitted
to the ordeal, and obligingly furnished him with a
column and a-half of mingled fact and fiction, .and
then asked him if knew where O'Rafferty was.

"O'Rafferty! I thought he went home with you!"
was the answer.

"But he came back some time ago, didn't he?"

"Not that I know of. In fact I'm sure he has
not come back. That blessed boat of his is lying
at Kanagawa, and if he were back he would be on
board her six times a day at least."

This struck the artist as passing strange. O'Rafferty had written him three months before from San
Francisco, stating in his own peculiar and figurative language that he 'was off to Japan on the track
of the squint-eyed limb of iniquity,' and as likely as
not further communications from him were now at
Gifford's London address.

He went out to Kanagawa and made inquiries,
and found matters to be as the newspaper man
had told him, for newspaper men sometimes do

speak the truth. From no source could he glean the slightest report or hearsay of O'Rafferty.

Next day he set forth on a quest which was to him desperately serious. It came to him as a revelation,—this fashion in which, when he thought of *her*, all his fibres thrilled and quivered, as tremble the pine-needles when the breeze is a-soughing among them. He noted the likeness as he glanced at the old gnarled tree that had witnessed their leave-taking.

He struck into the path that led from it to the wicket of the villa. It was tangled and hidden with the straw-coloured hues of sapless winter-grass and fringed with white-bearded Eulalia. His heart throbbed up into his mouth, and a rush of foreboding swept through him.

The road-way in front of the gate was rough and ragged and rutted, as if swept and torn by the rain-storms, while the wicket itself looked sallow and sickly like the barred up entrance to a ruin. He paused a moment and then he tried to run it aside in its groove. But it stood hard and fast and firm against the pressure of his fingers. At last it yielded slightly, and then as he brought the leverage of his shoulder to bear upon it, it ran back in its grooves with a harsh, grating jar, eloquent of lengthy disuse. He stooped and stepped within to find himself in a wildernèss. The paths were rutted and broken and covered with the débris of the autumn rains, the grass plots were all tangled and unkempt and littered with a confusion of pine-needles, bamboo-leaves and thatch from the eaves of the house. The villa itself was shut, mute and silent all round, with its *amado* streaked and marked and whitened by the fierce spitting showers that had beat upon them for a lapse of months.

Gifford tried to push the shutters apart and find a way within, but to no purpose. He then went to the bath-house, where he was more successful. He put his shoulder against the door, and its frailty yielded to the pressure. As he looked in upon its moist chilliness evening was darkening around. He stood there in gloomy silence with a dull pain somewhere in his side. There six months ago he had ———. And now he had returned to find something that looked worse than a tomb. He turned away and shut the door.

As he drove the wicket behind him with a strident groan, a great hawk flopped up from the water below, and slowly circled round overhead uttering a mournful 'Han! Han! Han!'

Gifford looked at it wickedly and with evil intent. He put his hand into the pocket on his thigh, and the bird seemed to take the hint, wheeling off over the cliff with a 'Han! Han! Han!' that sounded weird and threatening in the gathering gloom.

The artist paced along the path thinking. At present he was helpless, for he had brought no interpreter, never fancying for a moment that any go-between would be necessary. So the only thing to be done was to go back and institute inquiries from Yokohama or Tokyo.

"Oh! for five minutes of that mad Irishman!" he sighed.

Two days after this he established his head-quarters in the metropolis. He found a house ready furnished in Tsukiji, suitable in the matter of light, and in it he straightway encamped.

The first thing he did was to send off an agent, trusty, confidential, discreet and bilingual to Misaki to make inquiries.

That he was told might take a matter of three days. On the evening of the 30th,—it was now the 27th, progress was to be reported.

VII.

Meanwhile all that Gifford could do was to pos-
sess his soul in patience, to receive innumerable
calls, and accept or decline the invitations that poured
in upon him in half-dozens at each delivery. One
he did accept was from a Japanese Maecenas to a
Japanese dinner, pure and simple, on the 30th.
When his reply had gone he recollected with a
start that the 30th was the identical evening when
Mr. Kudo—that was how the ' trusty, confidential
etc.' was writ upon his card—was to wait upon him.
So after lunch on that day, he left instructions for
Kudo san to await his return if he called and
found him out.

Then the artist hied him forth to make the
best of the afternoon from a professional point of
view.   He meant to get a general notion of the
lie of the land he purposed to exploit professionally in the course of the next six months, for
it was Tokyo life, and Tokyo Street scenes that
were to be the backbone and main-stay of his next
Exhibition.

He first drove out to have a look at the Castle
wall with its moat flecked and dotted with wild-fowl,
its old white-washed ponderous gateways, and the
remnants of its battlements and turrets, and then he
fared North-Eastward to Asakusa.

It was cold—keenly cold—in the shade, although the winter sun shone brightly. The effects of his feeble strength were odd, so odd that once or twice Gifford stopped and brought his Kodak into operation. As he turned into the show-quarter of Asakusa he

was especially struck by its play on the features of three small gamins, and he immediately dismounted and annotated them with his camera for future reference. Then he made a detour towards the Sumida and finally came up into the temple of Kwannon through the gate next to the river.

The scene that faced him was unique. Round
everywhere were woods and trees that shivered in
their nakedness in spite of the make-believe warmth
from the rays of the winter's sun that flooded
all the open spaces.   To his right, the great square

massive temple-pile with its huge parabolic sweep
of sombre tiles, its heavy eaves, its great squat
pillars, its garish gables daubed in a red that
might have come from the shambles.   Then around
were countless tiny sheds and shrines, while on his

left rose the inevitable five-storied pagoda with its heavy-roofs topped with its caterpillar-like spire, seemingly in quest of shelter among the skeleton-like boughs of the trees, and there finding it not. Further down was the gateway, its huge goblin-like lantern depending from the ceiling of the doorway, and its heavy lumbering bulk of beams, and rafters, and eaves and roof projecting a huge stretch of icy shadow on the ground behind.

And up the middle-causeway resounded the 'patter! patter! patter!' of the *geta*-shod crowd, laughing and chattering and smiling, here resplendent in all the gorgeousness of silks and crêpes and there flapping the rags that scarcely hid its sores, like so many scare-crows at large. Four or five blind men came stumping along 'tap-tap-tapping' on the pavement in unison, and smiling and joking as if the world were really fair to their eyes. And then everywhere pigeons ran over the stones, with a 'coo-coo-coo' as they scurried in chase of the grains and tid-bits thrown to them by the throng. Occasionally they would spread their wings and whirr aloft gyrating, and perch cooing within the shelter of the sanctuary itself.

Within the great hall was a strange sight. It was simply topsy-turveydom run wild. Devils and Angels, the Princes and Powers of Darkness ranged cheek by jowl with Buddhas and Kwannon's, while money-changers, charm-sellers, and cake-vendors plied their vocation undisturbed by the worshipping throng that rubbed and wrung their hands and moved their lips in voiceless prayer as if they were puppets pulled by strings.

It was like the Middle Ages, the Arabian Nights, and a powerful nightmare all emptied into one big cauldron and well-mixed together.

Gifford looked at the scene with rising wonder and delight. At last he turned away, passed through the gate, and found himself in a long lane of little houses of red brick, every one of them a shop or booth, with a long paved way running between the rows.

Suddenly as he lounged along this paved way, he gave a great start and literally darted over to the front of a picture-shop. His sudden movement attracted the attention of the passing throng, always ready to take note of western men and their strange outlandish ways. Before he knew it, he had a knot of eager watchers around him. But he took little heed of that; he had eyes for one thing, and for one thing alone.

It was his own sketch of the old archer that faced him in the picture-stall.

There could be no doubt of it; it was not a copy; there was his own autograph in the corner. His first impulse was to regain it at any cost. But common-sense quickly interposed a veto. He knew 'ikura,' and he knew the Japanese numerals, and the sum of this knowledge would have sufficed to accomplish the bargain. But farther than that his Nihongo would not carry him, and the picture was a clue.

To follow it up an interpreter was necessary. So he carefully made note of the bearings of the shop, and walked away in search of some one who was bilingual.

Fortune this time was kind to him. About half-an-hour later he ran across the brass-buttons and queer-cornered flat cap of a student of the Imperial University. Gifford accosted him without demur. The student was courtesy itself.

"Yes, he understood English a little, and if he could render him any service he would be very pleased to do so."

Gifford briefly explained the necessary outlines of the matter, and they turned back to the street. They reached the spot and Gifford raised his finger to point out the sketch. But to his wonder it was gone. He looked around to make sure that he had not mistaken the shop. But nowhere in the neighbourhood was there any other such place ; and there, one on one side of it and one on the other, were the toy-stall and the *Shamisen* shop he had taken careful note of. In his excitement he began to think that fancy had been playing tricks with him.

He turned to the student and told him what had happened.

"Ha! Ha-a!" exclaimed the latter in sympathetic wonderment.

Then he asked the picture-dealer if she had not had such a sketch there half-an-hour ago.

The old woman bowed forward till she was double, and begged pardon. Then she went on to say that she had just sold the picture a few minutes before.

The student explained, and Gifford felt as if fortune were mocking him.

"To whom did you sell it?"

"An *O-josama* (young lady) came and paid 90 *sen* and took it away with her. But it was only a poor and shabby piece of work "—Gifford smiled grimly at this—" and there were many better ones in the shop. For example the pictures of these beautiful ———"

The student hastily interrupted the old woman's voluble flow of words and told her that the foreigner did not want any of these. But if she would answer a few questions she would be paid for her trouble.

Her eyes glistened with pleasure at this, and she again bowed and then reseated herself on her heels with her hands in her lap.

"Where had she got that picture?"

"Where? Oh! she had got that fairly enough. She had bought it at Haguchi, the pawn-broker's."

"When had she bought it?"

"Of when was it a thing? Perhaps of two months ago,—perhaps more."

"What was the young lady like who bought it? Of course she was a Japanese?"

"Yes, of course a Japanese *o-jo-sama;* a very pretty *o-jo-sama*, very tall in stature, with wonderful eyes and long lashes. And she was a very liberal young lady, for she did not bargain for the picture, but paid the first price asked for it at once."

This latter with a tinge of regret in the tone, no doubt at failing to make the most out of such a willing purchaser.

"But she perhaps wanted the picture at any price. Perhaps it was the picture of her own honourable father."

Gifford's heart gave a jump at this suggestion. What if the old woman's guess had all but grazed the mark! As likely as not it had been Ayame!

There was nothing more to be made out of this, so Gifford paid the old woman a few *sen*, and turned away. The student offered to come with him and explain things to him, and although Gifford wished much to be alone, he could not be so discourteous as to refuse the service so kindly proffered.

They went through the courtyard of the temple
again, and came out at the extremity of the Variety
Shows that here ring the margin of the pond and
stretch away as far as the eye can reach.   On
the one side, stunted, hungry-looking pines stood
shivering coldly in the biting wind in spite of
the sun that mocked them with a great glare of
warmthless light.   On the other side, the huge
unwieldly flags of the show-booths with   their
nightmarish barbaric legends were tugging and
jerking at their bamboo-poles, making them creak
and groan in their ring-bolts and fastenings.   Further along, beyond the weeping willows, a great
red-brick tower shot garishly aloft, its twelve rows
of windows glittering steely cold.

"As for this tower, what do you say to ascend it?" asked the student, turning to Gifford. "It is called the *Ryoun-kaku*, but it is usually known as the *Ju-ni-kai*, or the Twelve Storeys. From its top the view is fine, and besides there is a Beauty-show inside it?"

"A what?" said Gifford with astonishment.

"A Beauty show. Oh!" his companion went on with a laugh, "the beauties are not there in person. But one hundred of the most famous of the *geisha* of all parts of Tokyo have been photographed and their pictures have been placed in two of the flats, and every man who ascends the tower gets a voting-card with his admission-ticket, and he is supposed to vote for his favourite. It is really worth seeing."

Gifford under ordinary circumstances would have snatched at such an opportunity with the utmost eagerness. But at present he thought it only a bore. His mind was running on his sketch and the girl who had carried it off. Therefore he hated the hundred beauties of Tokyo. However he went, although moodily and as if in a dream.

They paid their 6 *sen* each, and received their admission-tickets and voting-cards. Then they stepped into the lift and were whirled away aloft into a still more numbing cold, and at last got out upon the platform.

It was an eerie prospect. The sun's disc was dipping grimly behind the Chichibu range, the great lumbering mountain mass that ran like a jagged retaining wall round the horizon sweep from West to North. In front of him was a thin gauzy bank of clouds, streaked with gorgeous golden bars. Up Fuji's flank, as he slowly sank from view, he threw one immense glorified pencil of ruddy light, that streamed away into nothingness in the void aloft, and left all the rest of the mountain in the threatening gloom of sullen menace. The eastern horizon seemed livid with fire and blood and heavy with smoke such as rises aloft and hangs over a captured town. To the North-East lay Tsukuba-san like a stranded leviatian, the uppermost swell of his back alone standing out clear beneath a patch of sky that looked simply appalling in its cold steely-gray pitilessness.

And over all the great expanse of gloomy sombre plain that spread in dank levels for miles on miles, the wind came piping and shrilling with all the cold of Yezo and the Frozen Sea rustling on its wings. And below southward, stretched a vast smoke-less sea of black-roofed buildings, like so many seeming rabbit-hutches, in irregular rows and mazes, except in one single streak, where a long symmetrical curve lined the course of the river reaches with its dusky hues. Further off was the

upper expanse of the Bay, crisped into ripples and
wavelets by the biting winter's wind.

Around the platform where they stood and
shivered, were immense brackets with huge electric
lamps depending from them, and on the telephone-
wires that ran below the breeze kept striking with
a weird, fantastic, tuneless, jarring hum. Some four
or five telescopes were placed in position, so as to
rake the circuit of the horizon. One of them was
trained upon the white-roofs and towers and spires
of the *Yoshiwara* below and seemed to reap for its
speculative owner a veritable copper harvest. As he
shivered, spite of his thick-wadded Japanese clothes,
he kept on proclaiming with chattering teeth that
through it you could see the *O-iran* at their toilette.
Notwithstanding the lashing wind only two men
failed to glue their eyes to the telescope to make
sure that the man had lied, and these two were
Gifford and the student.

"Ow!" said the latter shrugging up his shoulders
and contracting his chest, "But as for coldness, it *is*
cold! Don't you think that we have had enough?
What do you say to going down and seeing the
singers, and voting for your favourite?"

Gifford expressed his approval of the suggestion,
and down they went a seemingly endless series of
flights of steps never meant for long-legged Western
man. After passing a few refreshment rooms, and

what looked like a fragment of a Japanese *kwan-koba* (bazaar) broken adrift, with its dolls, it's baby's caps, its pinchbeck jewelry, its hairpins and contraptions of a nondescript hue, they reached the story that held the tail-end of the long coil of beauties that wound round several tiers of the structure in three closely-packed rows of photographs.

"Anyhow, those photos have been finished by a real workman," remarked Gifford, the artist coming uppermost in him. "Who is he?"

"Oh! that's Ogawa. That's his name there; those characters that you see below all the photographs."

He pointed to the 川 小, which Gifford noticed to be the only constant factor in the welter of characters that explained the purport of each individual picture.

"He's easily the king of his craft in Tōkyō," the student added. "The rest of the writing tells you about the girls. For example, here's" (at this point he leant over the rail and peered into one of the photos, for like most Japanese students he was near-sighted from much poring over hieroglyphics.) "For example, there's Kotsuma of the Massudaya of Shimbashi, Tokumatsu of the Shinakamuraya of Shimbashi, Wakazakura of the Yanagidaya of Yoshicho, Kaneko of the Owariya of the Yoshiwara, and so forth. But what do you think of them?

Which is your favourite? For I think foreign taste in the matter of beauty will be different from ours."

Gifford slowly pushed his way along the barrier, scrutinising one after another, and then he came back and declared for Kaneko of the Owariya.

"Ha! Ha!" said his cicerone. "That is strange! But let us see the storey below this."

They dived down another break-neck flight of steps, presumptively built in favour of babies, and the inspection of another batch of beauty began.

"By the way," remarked Mr. Tokiyeda—that was the name the student gave when Gifford asked him for it—"it will be better to go on to the last stage. There is a new and famous singer there, and all men speak of her. She was just come out, and is quite a *mezurashii mono* (a wonder), for she knows English."

"Indeed!" said Gifford roused into interest." "Let us see her, then."

"That is the famous O-sōyō, who manages many of the affairs of the singers," went on Tokiyeda san, pointing to an old lady of an uncertain age, who occupied a place in this Walhalla, much on the grounds that entitle the non-playing manager of Australian cricket-teams to pictorial immortality among the wielders of the willow.

"And here," he went on, "is what in my humble opinion is the Komachi of them all. But

what do *you* say? Ah!" he cried, rubbing his
hands in glee, as Gifford gave a great start when
his eyes lit on the photograph the other pointed
out. "I thought this face would astonish you; and
I am right!"

He was. For it was the face Gifford had dreamt
of for months, the face that had brought him back
to Japan, the face he had been hungrily and vainly
searching for for days.

It was Ayame herself.

VIII.

True to his word O'Rafferty boarded the *Komachi* next forenoon, and great was the joy of Koto at his appearance. His master resumed relations with him by putting a great knobby set of knuckles in front of his nose and requesting him "tu smell that."

"Now, thin," proceeded O'Raff, "if ye breathe a wurrud about what you see ye'll taste it, an' feel it, an' tingle from it all over! An' in case folks should overhear ye shpakin' in yer slape, ye'd best take yer honourable ripose on board the *Komachi* fur the rist av the week. Div yez moind me now?"

Koto-san professed to give heed unto him.

O'Rafferty then dived down the companion-way, with a bundle he had brought on board.

"Well, me bhoy!" he began with bluff heartiness, "an' how is it wid yez? Ye're a much sought-afther, if not exactly a popular maan in Tōkyō this mornin'. But we'll chate thim though, an' most av all that little scutt av an Ishida that's raised all this divil av a typhoon among the pōlicemen. I've brought yez av the sinews av war,—two thousand dollars in gould, an' notes an' drafts, fur variety is good."

He emptied his pockets on the cabin table as he spoke.

"An' here besoides," he went on with a kick at the bundle he had thrown on the floor, "is a Chaneyman's rig-out. Ye'd better go as that; it's the aisiest make-up wid yer oiye-brows all gone. The *Abyssinia* goes to-morrow at twelve; and here's yer ticket. Now, tell me pwhat sort av a toime ye've had. What do you think av the *Komachi.*"

"A first-rate craft. She's got the finest lines of any yacht I've seen in the East."

"Oh! but it's yerself that's a shport an' a pleasant-spoken gintleman!" cried O'Rafferty with delight, seizing his hand. "It's yersilf that's got the discarnment!"

"But she wants one thing to complete her," went on the other hesitatingly.

"*Pwhat?*" said O'Rafferty hastily dropping his hand and taking a step beckwards. "Pwhat were thim wurruds? Or do me ears desave me? One thing tu complete her! An pwhat moight that be, savin' the honour av yer thafeship?"

The latter section of these remarks was delivered with arms folded on the chest, and in the measured tones of the frigid politeness that preludes a storm.

"Well, it's only a trifle," said Akadani humbly. "But I've made a drawing of the *Komachi*, and—and don't your think this rather helps to set her off?"

He spread out a sheet of cartoon paper, with the *Komachi* perfect from truck to kelson. He pointed to her bows, with much deprecation. O'Rafferty deigned to inspect them with contracted and hostile eyes. The *this* was a figure-head; the design being the counterfeit presentment of the immortal Ono-no-Komachi herself.

O'Rafferty's brows unknit and a smile of childish joy flickered round the corners of his lips.

"Sorr!" he said with dignity and a bow to the other. "I wronged yez, and I apologise! Ye're a man av gaynius,—not tu say av ideas!"

Then he paused and looked closely at the drawing.

"An' it's mesilf that knows where the very thing

itsilf is tu be had fur the stealin', " he resumed at
last. " An' you'd be the very man fur the job, and
I'd give yez the commission, but under prisint
circumstances it 'ud be dangerous fur yez. Fur it's
yerself that's an artist all over,—even in thavin'."

Akadani did not seem to relish this left-handed
compliment very highly. But he was in no position
to resent it—at present.

"Now," said O'Rafferty, "I must be off. I've
got to watch the police an' chiefly that scutt Ishida.
I mane tu keep him in me oiye till ye're gone."

And O'Rafferty withdrew, still about the other's
business.

IX.

O'Rafferty got back to Tōkyō by an early afternoon train and, as luck would have it, had just
changed his raiment and appeared in public, when
he happened upon his man. He was on the point
of entering a tea-house in company with what
O'Rafferty incontinently set down as an 'another
scutt.' Wherein he was right.

Kudo the 'trusty, discreet, confidential,' des-
patched by Gifford to inquire, had gone, and inquired and returned. He had found the clue and followed it up without much difficulty, and was just on
the point of making his report, when a happy idea
occurred to him. Gifford was to pay him well.

But why not kill two birds with one stone? If properly engineered there was a silver-mine in the matter. Wherefore he diligently sought out Ishida Taro and made report unto him. And truly he was not without his reward.

The twain of them had turned into the *Fujiya* to talk over the matter at length.

O'Rafferty entered shortly after them and taking possession of the neighbouring room, placed his ear to the intervening *karakami*. To judge from the play of expression that scudded across the Irishman's speaking features, the following twenty minutes must have been pregnant with revelations.

"*Naruhodo! Naruhodo!*" said O'Rafferty to himself, punctuating his exclamations with vicious raps on the edge of the *hibachi* with his *kiseru* (Japanese tobacco-pipe). "Isn't he a swate morsel av iniquity now, that luvely limb av a Japanese ligislator? An' it's a hundred *yen*, the other spalpeen's tu get fur lyin' tu me pore frind Gifford. It 'ull be money wasted though. Faith! an' it's a clever maan he is, wid a foine head on his shoulders, is Gifford, but he needs a binivolint dispot tu luk afther his sowl's good. An' it's mesilf that u'll be Haroun-Al-Raschid tu the pore orphan painter maan!"

Here he sat bolt upright, finally knocked out the pipe and stuck it in his girdle.

"Unsatisfyin' thruck alongside av the dhuldeen!"
he muttered. "Now let me get hould av the loose
inds av the villany. Here's Gifford baadly hit wid
that sprig av a gurl he mistuk fur a landscape at
Misaki, six or sivin months since."

At this point in his reflections O'Rafferty paused
and winked knowingly. Then he resumed.

"An' she's shuk on him baadly too. An' I don't
wonder at thim, the both av thim bein' seemingly
possessed av the best av taste. Now thin, that
little bla'guard knows it's all *sayonara* tu him, if
they get the fortieth part av a wink av each other.
So he knows that Gifford's due at a Japanese faste,
where he'll thry in vain tu get dacently dhrunk,
an' the gurl's tu go there as the leading *geisha*
lady at eight o'clock. That's the original programme as far as me own limited intelligence can
even it out. An' thin, Ishida proposes tu come in
wid an amindmint, accordin' tu the rules av Parliamentary Procedure. An' it's mesilf that's just
the maan that intinds to burke it. An' musha, I
must after the futsteps av that weazened choild
av sin an' iniquity."

He hurried out and catching sight of the legislator
doubling the corner of the block, he made up upon
him and crossing to the other side of the street
lounged along, some little distance in his rear. As
he passed the clock-tower in Ginza, five sounded

forth from its bell. Darkness was closing in and
O'Rafferty rejoiced.

"It 'ull be aisier to act," he reflected. "Hullo!
he's in talk wid the *Keibu* (police-inspector). Begorrah I must see what *he'll* do ; he's me man
now!"

He allowed Ishida to vanish and followed the
other. After some little thought, and some fiddling
with the inevitable note-book, the inspector crossed
to a *Kobansho* (police sentry-box).

"Now thin, me frinds, out wid yer plans.
Arrah! now, an' there's wan av the pore un-
suspectin' victims himself."

Just then a two-men *jinrikisha* dashed past him,
almost bespattering him with the mud from its
wheels. Gifford wss the fare.

O'Rafferty got to the rear of the box and within
earshot.

"Faith!" he muttered after listening for five
minutes or so. "An' it's a well-devised *coup* the
inspector maan intinds. But he hasn't got her yet.
Now it's two hours yet tu wait."

He thought fora moment.

"No!" he said to himself. "It's not artistic.
The t'other way 'ull be more dramatic-loike.
It'll be loike old toimes, whin we wint shtalkin'
Pathans."

With this he tightened his belt, and hurried off

to a rickshaw-stand. He pounced upon one of the coolies and drew him aside. After a colloquy of a few minutes he wound up ;—

"Now, see you're there! It's not fifty *sen*, but three *yen* you'll get if the thing comes off as I tell you!"

X.

Gifford recovered his composure with a brave effort.

"Yes," he remarked, subsiding into a decent and decorous seeming of mild interest. "She *is* beautiful. But who is she?"

"Here her name is written;—Tsuyu of the Nakamuraya of Shimbashi. But of course Tsuyu is only her pen name."

"Her what?"

"Not her real name, you know. Don't you call it *nom de plume*, or pen-name? But of course as it is not a pen she uses, it will be right to say *shamisen*-name perhaps."

Tokiyeda-san laughed at his jokelet, and Gifford came in with the chorus. It was forced though, on his part, for he was thinking intently. He looked at his watch; it was now half-past four, and at five he was due in Kobikicho. There was no time now to rush of to the Nakamuraya, as it was the whole longing of his feet and soul to do. After the dinner though, ———.

He turned to the student, and telling him of his engagement, thanked him and took his leave. As he sped through the lanes and labyrinths he had eyes for nothing; the man was now supreme over the artist. Only as he neared his destination he

noticed a *Keibu* (police-inspector) in animated converse with a policeman at a *kobansho* (police-box). Round the corner was a tatterdemalion, with criminal written all over him, in nature's own plainest handwriting, greedily drinking in their words. In this case the thief was evidently getting points from the thief-catchers.

His two-legged steeds rushed him in through a gateway and up to a *genka* with the steps leading up to the *shoji* polished till they glowed with lustrous sheen. One of the men shouted out *O-tanomi-mosu,* and then together with his companion fell upon Gifford's shoe-laces like a spoiler

on the slain. Before they had unshod their fare,
almost wrenching his feet from his ancles in their
efforts, the *shoji* were slid back and a vision in a
medley of all the colours of the rainbow with a
sash tied in a great bow behind that looked like
a pair of gigantic butterfly wings in crêpe and gold,
went down on all-fours and its fore-head, and began
to flutter up and down as if pulled by strings.

" *Yoku irrashaimashita!* " it said and looked
up at him half-amusedly and half-coyly, and then
with something that was too marked for a smile,
and yet not sufficiently pronounced to pass for a
giggle, led him into the drawing-room. This fairy
struck him as being altogether too graceful for a
maid-servant; in his callow uninstructed ignorance
he set her down as the *O-jo-sama*, the daughter of
the house. He made a note of this, and later on
was laboriously piecing togther in sublimely ridiculous high-stepping Japanese a compliment to his
host on the beauty of his offspring when Providence
and circumstances interposed to save him from his
folly.

In the room, where his host stood to receive him,
he found a crowd of guests, some in the arm-chairs
and on the sofa in front of the sea-coal fire glowing and
crackling in the grate, and some standing in groups
on the heavy-piled carpet, and all in their stocking-
soles.

Mr. Okada, his host, introduced Gifford to His Excellency the Minister for This, the Consul for That, the Vice-Minister of one Department, the Chief Secretary to another, and then to a whole crowd of distinguished merchants, and to some artists. And most of them, bowed low as they shook hands, and said "*Hajimemashite; igo o kokoro-yasu.* . . . . (The beginning seeing; henceforth honorable intimately——)," and then they all stopped in the middle of the sentence, sucked in their breath, and tried to look pretty.

Then after ten minutes talk about the weather and earthquakes—the former trite and banal topic of discussion always admits of being judiciously seasoned with a modicum of seismology in Japan— Gifford heard a gentle rustle at his elbow and looked round and down to find an almost exact replica of the fairy that had ushered him into the room, offering him a cup of coffee. In the matter of height, and seemingly also of age, they were identical.

"Twins!" was the artist's unspoken commentary, as he took the proferred cup with the most winning smile he could conjure up. "Mine host is in luck."

The fairy received the empty cup on the tray and fluttered back with it to the side-board; her great wing-like bows of crêpe and gold rustling as they brushed against a chair-back. As Gifford followed her with artistic eyes, his brows went up in wonder.

"Triplets, by Jove!" he muttered to himself in an inaudible awe-struck whisper. "No wonder the Japanese newspapers print articles about the population-problem in their country!"

This remark was evoked by the presence of a third *O-jo-sama* in the corner assisting the other two in dispensing coffee and cakes. And just then, to make the seeming of things still more incredulous, a fourth damoselle of the same height, in the same garb, and of the same apparent fourteen springs, came flitting through one of the open *karakami* into the room.

"Poor Mrs. Okada!" groaned Gifford to himself sympathetically. "What sin can her parents or grandparents have committed to bring this awful retribution upon her!"

And then to crown all, a fifth, in all respects on a par with the others, entered to make the four a quintette. The artist felt as if pulverized into a moral and intellectual pulp. Dominie Sampson, he told himself, was the only man that could possibly annotate this text. It really, and truly, and indisputably was 'Pro-di-gi-ous.'

But at this point, Gifford's fore-scalp uncreased itself as a probable and highly luminous explanation of the puzzle struck him. It came into his mind

like a lightning-flash that in one respect at
least, it was with the lord and master of an
upper-class Japanese household as it is with an
ocean-tramp.

For in the law of Japan it stands written in un-
understandable chops that a man shall have but
one lawful wife in command, just as there is no more
than one skipper in charge of a steamer. But,
although a steamer has but one captain, and one
only, there is usually a first-mate, and a second-
mate, and a third-mate, and sometimes eke a fourth
to look after the boat's physical well-being and to
help to keep it spick and span and comfortable.
Applying this analogy to Mr. Okada's establishment, his quiver-full of seemingly simultaneous olive-
branches could be rationally accounted for.

However, Gifford thought well to fortify himself
with accurate data before launching his toilsomely
turned family compliment to puzzle his host's understanding. For truth to tell, it would have been as
easy to get at the true inwardness of what Gifford's
Nihongo was ettling at, as it would be to decipher
a batch of hieroglyphics scrabbled by an ancient
Egyptian just coming off an extended spree.

Wherefore Gifford turned to the English-speak-
ing Vice-Minister in his stocking soles beside him.

"What pretty daughters those are of Mr. Okada's!" he began rapturously.

Then he added in a subdued and questioning tone :—

"Of course, they are all Mr. Okada's, I presume?"

"Okada's daughters!" almost shouted the Vice, with a smile that was something more than audible. "Well, that is a joke! Okada san, do hear this?"

But Mr. Okada fortunately happened to be engrossed with a Foreign Plenipotentiary at the other end of the room, and did not notice.

"Okada's daughters!" went on the Vice-Minister, his waistcoat all rippled into creases with the quakings of his diaphragm. "Why, don't you know that Mr. Okada is, and always has been, that rare entity in Japan, a jolly bachelor? Okada's daughters, indeed! Why those are all *ōshaku* or apprentice-*geisha* from Shimbashi! They are here as Hebes in your especial honour. That is O-yen-san; she is the craze at present. All foreigners rave about her. Don't you think her really a beauty?"

He pointed to the girl that had last entered. She was wonderfully lithe and willowy for a Japanese maiden, with the oval face and long semi-Semitic cast of nose that in old Japan formed the very hall-mark of birth and breeding among women.

"Yes, she *is* pretty," said Gifford looking at her with admiration. "I must know her professimally by and bye."

"Professionally? queried his friend with a merry twinkle in his eye. "That is ambiguous enough for a non-committal diplomatic note. However I wish you luck, whichever way you mean it. As a matter of fact I don't know if many beauties in Tō-kyō can aspire even to hold a candle— that's the phrase isn't it?—to O-Yen-san. They say there's a full-fledged *geisha* out just a few days ago that's her superior in looks, but I can't speak with authority about her, as I haven't seen her yet. But I believe she's coming here this evening, later on. However, here comes our host to marshal us to the feast."

It was as he said. Mr. Okada approached and ushered them to the dining-room.

Gifford seated himself as directed, on the quilted silk cushion beside his host. He found himself separated by a good half-dozen places from the Vice-Minister, very much to his regret. For at the mention

of this new star risen among the singers, his heart
thumped against his ribs. What if it should be
——— ?

He scarcely dared to frame the thought. All
through the courses of the dinner he was on the
tenter-hooks of expectation. The Shimbashi *ōshaku*
had not half the charm for him they would have
had, had his thoughts been free for them alone. It
was with a listless abstraction amounting almost to
indifference that he noted their quaint ways, their
coyly mischievous glances, their elaborate and
deprecating politeness seasoned with no inconsider-
able spice of flippant impudence, the sly ogles they
cast on others as they filled up his tiny *saké*-cup,
with prostrations that seemed to protest that for the
nonce they existed but for him alone, and their
wonderful pose and gestures artificial and studied
to a degree that made them seem natural. Even
O-Yen-san, with all the petulant charm of a spoiled
beauty was to him only as a puppet or a lay-figure.
Small wonder it was, then, that after half-an-hour's
thankless attention, she left him with a pout to open
an elaborate flirtation with a Japanese-speaking
Chargé d' affaires.

It was only the fearful and wonderful ceremony
of cutting up the living *koi* and *tai* that was sufficiently potent to momentarily deflect his thoughts
from the channel they were coursing in.

In the middle of the dinner there was a mild commotion at one end of the long chamber where they sat. The forest of bamboos and pines in pots that made that region glow with a living green was thrust back, and with much ceremony a huge oblong block resting on four six-inch pedestals was placed at the unoccupied end of the rectangle formed by the guests. On it lay a *koi*, and beside it a knife and a pair of skewers. As Gifford looked at this performance, the *koi's* tail gave a stout and vigorous wallop of protest. The fish was alive beyond a doubt, though gasping with all the insufficiency of gills out of their element. Then as all laid down their chop-sticks and gazed door-wards in hushed expectancy, the head of a procession thrust itself through the entrance. First came one assistant, and then another, and then appeared the chief performer in the function—the officiating high-priest or executioner, the head cook.

And his coming was in state and stately. He was robed in flowing *hakama* and more than ell-wide sleeves, bulging out in gargoyles at the shoulder sizeable enough to obstruct the traffic of a narrowish street, and adorned as to his head with a lofty cap in the shape of a truncated cone fastened with ear-straps. As his acolytes bent and bowed backwards before him he advanced. And his gait was the goose-step of the German recruit.

Slowly and solemnly he advanced till he stood by
the block, and then he sank down on hands and
knees, and bent his forehead to the mats, and
bowed to the right and bowed to the left, and
bowed to his front, and then to make sure that he
had omitted no one at the corners he gave one
great final comprehensive salaam sweeping through
an arc of 270°. After this he remained still for a
few seconds, and then he bobbed up, settled his face
into the hard lines of one about to do stern and un-
relenting work, and seized the knife. He drew
squares and circles and all sorts of curves and
figures with the flashing steel on the board around
the fish and in the air above it, with a look
all grim and grisly. Then he seized the
skewers in his left and the silence in the hall grew
deeper.

"He mustn't touch the fish with his hands," explained Gifford's right hand neighbour in a whisper.

Nor did he. He made several passes with the
skewers, and then he caught the fish between them.
He held it there, stopping for a second to make
sure of his grip, and then the knife flashed, and a
long crunching '*z-i-i-ip*,' set teeth on edge, and made
back-bones arch between the shoulders. The knife
had shorn right along the spine of the victim
from head to tail, slicing off his dorsal fins together with the ridge of his back. Then came

slash after slash with lightning-like speed, and soon the poor *Koi* was nothing but the fragments of a corpse.

Shortly after, this performance was repeated on a *tai*, only at the end of the carving the executioner wound up with a brilliant piece of léger-de-main. He threw down his knife on its point on the block, and it stood with its blade quivering in the midst of the dismembered victim. Then he spun the skewers into the air, and down they came on their sharp ends, crossing each other opposite the perpendicular knife, and forming with the block as a base-line an almost perfect equilateral triangle. It was a workmanlike trick, featly and deftly done.

Then the performer bowed low as before, and gathering himself up, slowly goose-stepped it from the room followed by a whirlwind of hand-claps. His juniors took up the block and bore off its burden to the pot.

While it was being cooked, two *geisha* who had appeared upon the scene, produced their *shamisen* and lifted up their voices, and first one *Oshaku*, and then another, and finally the whole bevy of five did even as the daughter of Herodias did before Herod the King.

Gifford, spite of himself was charmed. But yet he was poignantly disappointed. For the *geisha*, albeit passing lovely, were none of them the one his eyes longed for. He turned to his neighbour and asked which of them was the famous *débutante*. Of course he was pretty well aware what form the answer would take.

"Neither of them; she will appear later on, I believe. Being all the rage now, she has engagement over-lapping engagement, and cannot get free to come here before eight. But," here he looked at his watch, "she must be here presently. Hark! Didn't you hear the jingle of rickshaw wheels? That's most likely she."

Just then the host rose and left the room. . In a few minutes he returned, evidently ruffled and upset, though he struggled not to shew it.

"A strange thing has happened," he explained in Japanese. "O Tsuyu had just arrived when two policemen arrested her. They say it is for wilful fire-raising, burning down Ishida's house. It is very strange and at the same time very bothering and tiresome!"

He said nothing further, but devoted himself anew to his guests. But somehow things began to flag. Less than half-an-hour later, Mr. Okada was again called from the room. This time he returned with a note for Gifford.

When the latter took it, '*Urgent, Very Urgent,*' three-times underlined, met his eyes on the envelope. With an apology he opened it. It was

dated from his house in Tsukiji, at 8.15 p.m. It
ran:—

*Please come here without delay, as you are wanted
on the most pressing of business.*

      Your obedient servant,

        I. Kudo.

There was no resisting that. He explained to
his host, and took his leave as decently as he
could. His cook was at the door; he had brought
the note, but the only information he could give was
that the gentleman who give it him had told him to
run all the way. "Which he had humbly done"
he panted.

As the artist got into his *kuruma*, he
noticed a commotion among the bushes in the
garden. The servants were dragging something
or somebody from there forward into the light.
Gifford could just see that it was one in coolies
clothes, tied and bound like a captured malefactor.
Also with a gag in his mouth. Just then his men
dashed off and whisked him through the gateway
into the night, while the cook came puffing and
panting behind.

XI.

Since the 26th of December, Tokyo had gone wild over a famous new singer that had made her *début* on that evening. When Kotake of the Nakamuraya of Shimbashi had paid O-Tsuyu-san five hundred *yen* down, for a three year's contract, with an implied understanding that the recruit was ultimately to assume the headship of the house, she told herself that she had done a good stroke of business. But how good, even Kotake herself had had no adequate notion.

O-Tsuyu had been photographed forthwith and entered among the competitors for the suffrages of

the Tōkyō gallants in the *Ju-ni-kai* of Asakusa.
She had been zincographed in the *Yamato*, and the
Yomiuri, while the *Miyako* had issued a special
supplement devoted *in laudem* O Tsuyu alone.
The wicket of the Nakamuraya was eternally 'click,
click, clicking' behind messengers from tea-houses
and elsewhere requesting the honour of the Honourable Miss Tsuyu's attendance at feasts and
functions of all kinds. She found herself in a
whirl of overlapping engagements. Hence it was
that when Mr. Okada had called her to his
house for the evening of the 30th, she had been
obliged to decline. Then when he had become
insistent and pressing, and offered a *hana* of more
than lordly proportions, Kotake had attempted to
arrange a compromise for her, and had succeeded.
O-Tsuyu-san was to go from 8 to 10 P.M.

And punctual to her engagement she was at the
door at the appointed hour. It had been the jangle
of her *jinrikisha's* wheels that had caught the ear
of Gifford's neighbour. And it was because he had
to enter without her after all, that Mr. Okada was
put out so sorely. For when he appeared on the
door-step a strange thing was happening.

O-Tsuyu's jinrikisha-man had just dropped the
shafts of his vehicle, and had got out between them
to assist her to alight, when a police inspector and
a constable popped out from the shade of the trees

and called upon her to stop. She looked up with
a cry of surprise.

"Stop!" said the *keibu* (inspector) coming forward and putting his hand upon her arm. "I arrest
you, Tanaka Ayame, now known as O-Tsuyu of
the Nakamuraya of Shimbashi for the arson of Mr.
Ishida Taro's house in Kojimachi on the evening of
the 24th."

Then he proceeded in a quieter and semi-un-
official tone;—

"I am sorry to trouble you, but I must do it.
It is my orders."

At this point Mr. Okada came on the scene, and
peremptorily demanded the meaning of it all. The
inspector went up to him and saluted. In a low
voice he gave an explanation, interrupted by impatient '*He! He!* s' from his auditor. Then he
turned round and called to the coolie to drive back.

But no coolie was there to receive the instructions.
He had gone aside among the bushes; when the
keibu raised his voice and called for him sharply,
he at last sprang nimbly forward, after rustling
among the bushes for a few seconds like a dog on
the scent. He jumped into the shafts and made
ready for the word to go. The *keibu* got into
another *kuruma*, and the constable into another, and
then with O-Tsuyu as a prisoner between them
they set forth in Indian file.

They passed though the gateway at a walk, and
then the *keibu* gave the word to go quickly and off
they sped into the darkness.

For several hundred yards they skimmed along
with a rush. Then just as they were rounding a
corner at full tilt, the right-wheel of the *keibu's*
jinriki seemed to jolt against a regular boulder.
Up that side of the rickshaw went, while the sparks
flew like fire-flies on a summer night and at the
same moment the drawer seemed to stumble over
another obstruction. It was in vain that O-Tsuyu's
kurumaya stretched out his hand to steady the
swaying vehicle. Up, and up, its right side went,
and over it lurched with a crash, spilling the
keibu and the coolie a-top of each other in the way.
The second coolie pulled up so abruptly that the
third man ran into his vehicle before he could
moderate his pace, and he and his jinriki and its
fare were tumbled in a heap above the inspector.

The second man gave but scant heed to their
plight. He dodged nimbly round the wreck in the
frosty road, and leaning forward in the shafts,
rushed on like a two-legged whirlwind. By the
time the *keibu* had disentangled himself and his
sword from the heap of confusion a-top of him, his
prisoner was racing down towards the vanishing
point in the curve of the alley-way. He shouted
and hallooed for the *kurumaya* to stop, but he

shouted and hallooed in vain. Then he dashed off in chase as fast as he could run. But not a track or trace of the fugitive rickshaw was to be seen.

The *keibu* roused all the men at the sentry-boxes he passed, and soon a whole *posse* was in pursuit. But to no purpose.

At last, as they neared the canal towards Tsukiji, one of the constables pointed to something floating in the water. They went down and hooked it and pulled it to the bank. It was a *kuruma*, minus one wheel, and in it were a shawl and a pair of *geta* such as *geisha* wear.

XII.

Gifford with his two men *jinrikisha* far outpaced the cook. In ten minutes he was at the door of his house, fumbling for his latch-key and finding it not, because he had left it behind when he started out early in the afternoon. He looked up to find all the front rooms of the building in darkness, excepting only one of the upstairs suite where the gas was burning at a dim and religious low pressure.

"Confound it!" he muttered to himself. "What's to be done? Perhaps the back door is open."

He jumped down the steps and hurried round to the kitchen. His surmise was correct; the door was open. He entered briskly, tripping over pots and pans in his progress. A figure like a wayside rickshawman was sitting by the fire, smoking a European pipe. It turned round, and stretching out a hand addressed him.

"Well, me bhoy! It's mesilf that am glad tu see yez!"

"O'Rafferty!" shouted the artist,—"or the Devil! What the mischief are you doing in this masquerade?"

"This *how much?* What language is that?" queried the coolie extricating his fingers from Gifford's clasp. "Excuse me for not risin' tu resave yez and wilcome yez wid all the honours av war, but I've bruk me fut again. It's as bad as El Teb!"

"What *have* you been doing?"

"Transactin' a thrifle av business!"

"Have you got your money?"

"I have! An' now I'm purtectin' the thafe from the consiquence av his croimes. He's a bit av a shport, I would have yez know. An' the foinest av all, *she's* all right!"

"She! Who?" cried Gifford excitedly, jumping up from the chair he had straddled in front of O'Rafferty.

"Who? Why the *Komachi* av course!" replied the Irishman in an injured tone of wonder.

"Oh the *Komachi* be ———!"

And Gifford reseated himself with a thud on the cane-bottom.

O'Rafferty's eyelids came together and his pupils contracted to pin-points.

"Me frind Gifford!" he said slowly. "Thim's harsh wurruds, an' I'll make bould tu ask yez tu widdraw thim. If 't wern't a joyful occasion I'd perhaps resint thim."

"I beg your pardon, old man!" said Gifford meekly, catching him by the hand. "But I'm in a great bother about some other *she* to-night, and I want you to help me. Will you?"

"Will I? Who are yez askin'? Av course I will. But who is *she?*"

"Who? Why, Ayame, the girl we met at Misaki. Who else could it be?"

"Whe-ew! Then I *was* roight afther all, although ye threw logs av wood at me fur makin' baseless insinuations. Well, what about her?"

"I want you to go right off with me to see her."

"H'm! that's a biggish order. We'll have to foind her first."

"I know where she is to be found!"

"The Divil you do! An' whince came yer information?"

"I found it out myself, five hours ago. I saw her photograph in the *Ju-ni-kai*. She's in one of the *geisha* houses in Shimbashi."

"Whe-ew!" again whistled O'Rafferty. "It's a moighty 'cute an' clever man yez are! But you'll not foind her in any *geisha* house in Shimbashi at this hour, or indade at any hour to-noight at all, at all! An' so yez better make up yer moind to help *me* wid a little job I wanted yez fur expressly."

"Not be found in Shimbashi? Why?"

"Because in the first place, it's new year's toime and wid all the *geisha* it 'ull be 'twang! twang! twang!' and caterwaul till twelve o'clock, an' it's now only noine. An' in the nixt the idintical young lady in question was arristed about an hour ago fur wilful fire-raisin' and burnin' down the house she was tu live in wid her prospective husband, Ishida Taro."

"What do you mean, man? Explain, will you, for God's sake!"

"All right! but be aisy now. Listen!"

O'Rafferty refilled his pipe with the most provoking coolness, crossed one nude knee over the other, and kept Gifford on tenter-hooks for a quarter of an hour with a long rambling circumstantial narrative garnished with an abundance of Milesian figures.

At the end of it Gifford jumped up excitedly.

"Good Heavens! What's to be done?" he cried striding up and down the kitchen.

"Done? Nothing, till to-morrow."

"And the poor girl in jail all the time!"

"Don't take on about that!" replied O'Rafferty soothingly. "She'll be quite comfortable. Sit down, will yez an' listen tu me. I'm in difficulties too."

"How?" said Gifford absently.

"I've just shtolen a model fur a figure-head fur the *Komachi* an' I want you to take charge av it."

"Stolen! Where from?"

"A tay-house. I had tu tie a maan up wid shtring and fill his mouth wid a hankerchief and throw him into the bushes tu pirpitrate me purpose. It's moighty cowld there, so I want yez to sind a messenger tu tell thim to let him loose. But that's only a throifle and not the main pint at all, at all. I want yez tu keep this model fur me in yer house, because bein' a furrin' house, thim divils av pōlice can't come afther me widout a warrant. I want to show yez it. But ye don't appear to take much interest in the mather!"

"Man! under present circumstances how *can* ye expect me to think of a model for the *Komachi's* figure-head?" said Gifford with an impatient gesture.

"I'm thinking that when ye've seen it, it's just on nought else yer thoughts 'ull run the whole av this blessed noight," replied O'Rafferty very slowly and very drily. "But anyhow, come an' have a luk at it!"

He rose, and beckoned Gifford to follow him. He toiled painfully up the stairs and entered the front-room and turned up the gas. He then hobbled to the door that opened into the room beyond.

"Well," said Gifford wonderingly, "you seem to know the geography of my own house uncommonly well. You ."

"'Sh!" interrupted O'Rafferty, mysteriously placing his fore-finger on his lip.

He knocked at the door, and then opening it gingerly he pushed Gifford into the room. There was a death-like pause, a hurried sweep of garments across the floor, and then a brace of thrilling exclamations rang out together :—

"*Charles!*"

"*Ayame!*"

O'Rafferty quickly shut the door. Then leaning back against the post and holding the knob in his right hand he held up his left warningly, and with a wink of mischief addressed himself apologetically and confidentially to an invisible audience in space.

"Ye see it's a mane artist that shpoils everything by lavin' nothing tu the play av the imagination!"

ERRATA.

Pages.	Lines.
251	13 :—Save.
253	6 :—Most.
255	11 :—*After* if *insert* he.
277	13 :—*For* your *read* you.
281	1 :—*For* dhuldeen *read* dhudeen.
282	16 :—*For* wss *read* was.
282	23 :—*For* fora *read* for a.

www.ingramcontent.com/pod-product-compliance
Lightning Source LLC
Chambersburg PA
CBHW021215270326
41929CB00010B/1134